HOW GOOD IS YOUR IQ?

ABOUT THE AUTHOR

Nathan Haselbauer is the president and founder of the International High IQ Society. The International High IQ Society, the fastest growing high IQ organization in the world, was founded in New York City in 2000 to enable bright people from around the world to come together on the Internet. The Society welcomes people from all walks of life who have an IQ in the top five per cent of the population and who want to be part of the Society's global community. The Society is unique in that its combined membership includes people of all ages, races, and professions, and literally spans the globe.

Membership in the International High IQ Society is open to persons who score within the top five per cent of the general population on one of the Society's admissions tests. There is no other qualification for membership.

The tests can be found on the Internet at www.highiqsociety.org or by sending an e-mail to membership@highiqsociety.org.

HOW GOOD IS YOUR IQ?

Nathan Haselbauer

RIGHT WAY

Constable & Robinson Ltd
3 The Lanchesters
162 Fulham Palace Road
London W6 9ER
www.constablerobinson.com

First published in the UK by Right Way,
an imprint of Constable & Robinson, 2009

A copy of the British Library Cataloguing in Publication Data is available from the British Library

ISBN: 978-0-7160-2214-5

Printed and bound in the EU

1 3 5 7 9 10 8 6 4 2

CONTENTS

ACKNOWLEDGEMENT

Nathan Haselbauer would like to thank Craig Varsa for his help with this book, and particularly for his work on Multiple Intelligences in Chapter 3.

INTRODUCTION

The earliest organized thought on the concept of intelligence testing began with a nineteenth-century British scientist named Sir Francis Galton. After Charles Darwin published *The Origin of Species* in 1859, Galton got the idea to investigate the relationship between heredity and human ability. The prevailing zeitgeist of the time was that the human race had only a handful of really intelligent people and a small number of mentally deficient people, while the majority of the population fell within a narrow band of intelligence. Galton believed that mental traits were based on physical factors and were inherited traits, just like eye colour and blood type. Galton's work was also influenced by Belgian statistician Quetelet, who was the first to apply statistical methods to the study of human characteristics. Quetelet first postulated the concept of a normal distribution of intelligence on a bell curve. Galton published his ideas in a book titled *Hereditary Genius*, which is considered the first scientific investigation into the concept of intelligence.

The first to devise a test to assess human intelligence, however, was French psychologist Alfred Binet. Binet was interested in developing a test to measure intelligence in children. He started trial-and-error testing with Parisian students to determine what the normal abilities would be for a certain age and identify those who were below the norm. In 1904, the French government commissioned Binet to find a method of differentiating between children who were intellectually normal and those who were inferior. The purpose was to put the inferior children into special schools where they would receive additional schooling. Binet's test was called the Binet Scale and it is at this time that the phrase "intelligence quotient", or "IQ", first appeared.

An American school administrator, H.H. Goddard, found out about Binet's work in France and decided to use his test to screen students for his school. After knowledge of Goddard's use of Binet's test spread across the country, a professor at Stanford, Lewis Terman, worked on revising Binet's test. In 1916, Terman published his seminal work, the *Stanford Revision of the Binet-Simon Scale of Intelligence* (also known as the Stanford-Binet), which quickly became the gold standard for intelligence testing in the United States for the next several decades.

When America entered World War I the U.S. Army was faced with the problem of sorting huge numbers of draftees into various Army positions. To solve this problem, the Army put together an ad hoc committee of the top psychologists in the country to design an intelligence test for new recruits. Lewis Terman was on the Army's committee and they adopted a standard test for all new recruits, which, by 1919, was taken by nearly two million soldiers. The Army's test put intelligence testing on the map and its popularity exploded shortly thereafter.

Building on the Army's popular intelligence test, many companies began their own forms of intelligence testing to determine potential new employees, who to promote, and so on. The tests also quickly became ubiquitous in education; by the 1950s nearly every school district in the United States was conducting some form of intelligence testing.

By the 1960s doubts were raised about the cultural biases inherent in intelligence tests and the New York City Board of Education eliminated all IQ testing in their school system. Many other school districts followed suit, blaming racial and culturally loaded questions for large gaps in scores amongst certain groups and ethnicities.

By the 1980s ideas on intelligence testing were shifting, with Howard Gardner coming up with the concept of multiple intelligences. Gardner defined seven distinct intelligences: logical-mathematical, linguistic, spatial, musical, bodily-kinesthetic, interpersonal, and intrapersonal intelligences. His work in multiple intelligences quickly filtered through the industry and many tests were remodeled to reflect the new views on intelligence. Gardner's ideas gave birth to the modern intelligence test and these began to find their way back into the educational system in many forms, from IQ tests to standardized tests like the SATs.

Modern psychology has refined the intelligence test to a degree never thought possible even fifty years ago. Many consider the IQ test not only the most important achievement in the field of psychology, but one of the crowning achievements in modern society. In 1989, the American Academy for the Advancement of Science listed the IQ test among the twenty most significant scientific discoveries of the century along with nuclear fission, DNA, the transistor, and flight.

1

ASSESSING YOUR SOCIAL INTELLIGENCE

Asssessing your social intelligence

The concept of social intelligence, originally coined by E.L. Thorndike in 1920, referred to a person's ability to understand and manage other people, and to engage in adaptive social interactions. More recently social intelligence has been redefined to refer to the individual's fund of knowledge about the social world.

The professional view of social intelligence has taken on many forms since inception. Initially, pioneers like Thorndike described social intelligence as, "the ability to understand and manage men and women, boys and girls – to act wisely in human relations." The definition of social intelligence was further refined as the ability to get along with people in general, as well as knowledge of social matters and susceptibility to stimuli from other members of a group, as well as insight into the temporary moods or underlying personality traits of strangers.

Defining social intelligence is much easier than measuring it, however. Tests of social intelligence are notoriously difficult to design, and translating the abstract definitions of social intelligence into a standardized test for measuring individual differences is far from an exact science. In fact, the difficulty discriminating between social intelligence and raw IQ has led to declining interest in the overall concept of social intelligence.

The following analysis presented here will give you an idea of your social effectiveness, through a series of ten interpersonal situations.

How to take the test

Here are eight situations that measure different aspects of social intelligence. Read through each situation and then look at the responses posed in the table. Each of these represents how you might respond to the situation. Your objective is to rate each of the responses in terms of its effectiveness.

The rating scale goes from one to five, with one being very ineffective and five being the ideal response.

1	Very ineffective
2	Fair
3	Neutral
4	Effective
5	Very Effective

BEGIN TEST

Situation 1

Professional/Work related

You are a manager of a team of sales representatives. One of your employees, Rick, has been with the company for a long time and has been a capable worker. One morning, you get a call from one of Rick's long-time customers and they explain that Rick was rude to them on the phone, even though he's been fair with them in the past. You call Rick into your office and explain the situation and discipline him accordingly. While you are doing so, Rick says, "I don't like this company and think maybe I should quit."

Below are five potential responses to Rick's situation. Rate each one according to how effective you think it would be.

Response number	Your potential response
1	I think you should quit then!
2	If that is what you feel you must do, then do so.
3	It sounds like you are upset right now, why don't we continue this discussion later?
4	You're completely overreacting here!
5	You've been with the company a long time, this isn't worth quitting over. Let's try to work this out.

Response number	Very ineffective	Fair	Neutral	Positive	Very effective
1					
2					
3					
4					
5					

Situation 2

Professional/Work related

You have been working at your company for ten years and have not had a history of leaving work early. You have a doctor's appointment that requires you to leave work a half-hour earlier than scheduled. Instead of letting your boss know you have to leave early, you decide to leave unnoticed and hope nobody sees you. Your boss finds out that you left early and the next day he comes into your office and asks what happened.

Below are five potential responses to your boss. Rate each one according to how effective you think it would be.

Response number	Your potential response
1	I'm sorry, it won't happen again.
2	Look, I never leave early, will you stop bothering me.
3	I had an appointment that couldn't be missed. I'm sorry for not telling you.
4	It couldn't be helped.
5	I understand you're upset, but I had a personal issue to attend to.

Response number	Very ineffective	Fair	Neutral	Positive	Very effective
1					
2					
3					
4					
5					

Situation 3

Relationship related

You and your spouse have been married for ten years. Recently, you've been having more arguments than in the past. You went away for a three-day business trip and did not contact her while you were away. When you come home from your trip your spouse says to you, "How come you didn't call me while you were away? Do you still love me?"

Below are five potential responses to your spouse. Rate each one according to how effective you think it would be.

Response number	Your potential response
1	I don't want to talk about it.
2	I was working very hard and did not have time to phone you.
3	I'm vey tired now, I've been travelling all day. Can we talk about this tomorrow?
4	Yes, I still love you. I'll try harder in the future.
5	Why didn't you try to call me, maybe it's you who doesn't love me?

Response number	Very ineffective	Fair	Neutral	Positive	Very effective
1					
2					
3					
4					
5					

Situation 4

Relationship related

You come home from work and your spouse says to you, "We never do anything together any more and you never want to do anything that I want to do. This marriage is falling apart and it's all your fault!"

Below are five potential responses to your spouse. Rate each one according to how effective you think it would be.

Response number	Your potential response
1	It's as much your fault as it is mine.
2	How about we do whatever you want this weekend?
3	Hang on a second! You never want to do what I want either.
4	I'm sorry, but I don't agree.
5	Sometimes I feel the same way as you do.

Response number	Very ineffective	Fair	Neutral	Positive	Very effective
1					
2					
3					
4					
5					

Situation 5

Parenting related

You find out that your nine-year-old daughter has broken her finger while playing with her friends at the local playground. You arrive at the hospital and find her crying. She says, "My finger is broken, do I have to go to school this week?"

Below are five potential responses to your daughter. Rate each one according to how effective you think it would be.

Response number	Your potential response
1	You should be more careful.
2	This is your fault and I'm not letting you miss school. I'm sorry.
3	I'm glad that you're okay, but I don't want you missing school.
4	Didn't I tell you to be more careful in the playground? Now you've learned your lesson I hope.
5	If the doctor advises taking time off, then it's okay. I'm just glad you're okay though.

Response number	Very ineffective	Fair	Neutral	Positive	Very effective
1					
2					
3					
4					
5					

Situation 6

Professional/Work related

You are taking clients out to a business lunch to discuss a proposal. The clients have a very small budget and you don't feel that they are worth spending much time on. Your food hasn't arrived in quite some time and you cannot find your server. A different server walks by your table and you ask him where your food is. The server says, I'm not your server, it's not my problem."

Below are five potential responses to the server. Rate each one according to how effective you think it would be.

Response number	Your potential response
1	I want to talk to your boss right now.
2	I know, but we're in a hurry. Please find him and send him over.
3	You must be having a rough day today.
4	I know you're busy too. If you happen to see him, could you ask him to come over?
5	That's not how you speak to customers.

Response number	Very ineffective	Fair	Neutral	Positive	Very effective
1					
2					
3					
4					
5					

Situation 7

Neighbour related

Your neighbour knocks on your door and in a stern voice says to you, "Your stupid dog has been digging in my garden."

Below are five potential responses to your neighbour. Rate each one according to how effective you think it would be.

Response number	Your potential response
1	I'll keep a better eye on him. I'm sorry.
2	You don't have the right to talk to me this way.
3	He's just a dog, not a human. Relax.
4	You look after your pets and I'll take care of mine.
5	These things happen with pets.

Response number	Very ineffective	Fair	Neutral	Positive	Very effective
1					
2					
3					
4					
5					

Situation 8

Community related

You are driving in your car and get into a minor accident. No one is injured and there is only very minor damage to both vehicles. It's apparent that the accident was caused equally by both drivers. The other driver gets out of his car, and starts yelling, "You idiot, look what you've done to my car! This is all your fault!"

Below are five potential responses to the other driver. Rate each one according to how effective you think it would be.

Response number	Your potential response
1	If anything, it's all your fault.
2	We'll let the insurance companies settle the dispute.
3	It wasn't all my fault so calm down.
4	I'm sure we can resolve the issue, there is no need for yelling.
5	If you had been paying more attention this wouldn't have happened.

Response number	Very ineffective	Fair	Neutral	Positive	Very effective
1					
2					
3					
4					
5					

How to score this test

When you have completed all the situations use the answer key to find out how the experts would rate your decision. If you selected the same answer as the experts, award yourself three points, and if you chose an answer that is one off on either side award yourself one point.

For example, for response one, if you chose Very Effective and the answer key also had Very Effective, give yourself three points. If you chose Neutral and the answer key had either Fair or Positive, award yourself one point. Otherwise you receive no points for that response.

Answer key

Situation 1

Response 1	Very ineffective	
Response 2	Very ineffective	
Response 3	Neutral	
Response 4	Very ineffective	
Response 5	Very effective	

Situation 2

Response 1	Neutral	
Response 2	Very ineffective	
Response 3	Positive	
Response 4	Very ineffective	
Response 5	Very effective	

Situation 3

Response 1	Neutral	
Response 2	Very ineffective	
Response 3	Neutral	
Response 4	Very effective	
Response 5	Very ineffective	

Situation 4

Response 1	Very ineffective	
Response 2	Positive	
Response 3	Neutral	
Response 4	Very ineffective	
Response 5	Neutral	

Situation 5

Response 1	Very ineffective	
Response 2	Very ineffective	
Response 3	Positive	
Response 4	Very ineffective	
Response 5	Very effective	

Situation 6

Response 1	Very ineffective	
Response 2	Neutral	
Response 3	Very ineffective	
Response 4	Neutral	
Response 5	Very effective	

Situation 7

Response 1	Very ineffective	
Response 2	Positive	
Response 3	Very ineffective	
Response 4	Very ineffective	
Response 5	Neutral	

Situation 8

Response 1	Very ineffective	
Response 2	Neutral	
Response 3	Very ineffective	
Response 4	Positive	
Response 5	Very ineffective	

Determining your level of social intelligence

If your total score was between 110–120 you tend to handle situations very professionally. This score is in the top 10 per cent.

If your total score was between 100–109 you did a good job handling the situations, although it's possible a few of your responses may have resulted in conflict.

If your total score was between 90–99 there's a good chance many of your responses created conflict.

If your total score was between 80–89 you are definitely arguing and creating conflict.

If your total score was 79 or lower you are at the low end of the scale and tend to have very argumentative interactions in these situations.

Further reading

History and Social Intelligence by Harry Elmer Barnes
The Power of Social Intelligence by Tony Buzan

2

ASSESSING YOUR EMOTIONAL INTELLIGENCE

Assessing your emotional intelligence

Emotional intelligence is essentially the ability to understand your emotions and those of people around you. There are personal characteristics of emotional intelligence which are responsible for the way you behave, how you feel, how you relate to others, how well you do your job, and how healthy you are.

Knowing your emotional intelligence gives you the opportunity to seek out jobs that naturally fit you, puts you in a position to be with people you are compatible with, and can help you understand the specific things that cause you stress. People with a high emotional intelligence tend to be healthier, less depressed, more productive at work, and have better relationships.

Not knowing your emotional intelligence tendencies can result in being incompatible with others, not being happy or succeeding at your job, and chronic health problems.

There is a long-standing belief that IQ is the best measure of human potential. However, new research in the past decade has found that emotional intelligence might be a better predictor of success. Those with a high IQ are not necessarily emotionally intelligent. Possessing a good memory, or good problem-solving skills, does not mean you are capable of dealing with emotions or motivating yourself. Highly intelligent people may lack the social skills that are associated with high emotional intelligence, but, the combination of a high intelligence and low emotional intelligence is relatively rare in society. It's quite possible to be both intellectually and emotionally intelligent.

Having a high intellect is certainly advantageous in life, but to be able to do things like identify and label your feelings, to be empathic, to delay gratification, and to be able to read and interpret social cues requires a high emotional intelligence.

How to take the test

The Emotional Intelligence Test comprises 26 scenarios, including some from the social intelligence and assertiveness tests. All these combine to form a larger, more thorough test of overall emotional intelligence.

To take the test, read the scenario and answer it according to your most likely reaction. There is a tendency to try to choose the "correct" answer or what you think the test designer thinks is the correct answer. It is important to answer the questions honestly if you want an accurate appraisal of your emotional intelligence.

There is no time limit for this test.

BEGIN TEST

1. You are leaving work for the weekend in a great mood. The work week went very well and you have some special plans this weekend that you are really looking forward to. As you leave work and get in your car, you notice that it won't start. After a while you finally get it started, but now you feel:

   ☐ A. Upset. You assume your car could have any number of costly problems.

   ☐ B. Concerned about your car, but still in a good mood overall. You just make sure to call a mechanic first thing in the morning.

   ☐ C. You still feel good about your day, but know you will have to get your car looked at eventually.

   ☐ D. You decide to ignore your car completely, because you don't want to ruin your good mood.

2. You are driving in your car and get into a minor accident. No one is injured and there is only very minor damage to both vehicles. It's apparent that the accident was caused equally by both drivers. The other driver gets out of his car, and starts yelling, "You idiot, look what you've done to my car! This is all your fault." You:

   ☐ A. Tell the driver to calm down since it was only a minor accident and no one was hurt.

   ☐ B. Explain to the driver that the fault rests with both of us and we should let the insurance companies figure it out.

   ☐ C. Patiently wait for the driver to calm down before you try to exchange information.

   ☐ D. Start yelling back at the driver, insisting that if it's anyone's fault here it's obviously his

3. A friend invites you to a party. Although you think a few friends of yours will be attending, you know that most of the people at the party are people whom you have never met before. You:

- ☐ A. Decide to stay home, even though you wanted to go.
- ☐ B. Go to the party but only talk with the people you already know.
- ☐ C. Talk mostly with your friends unless a stranger approaches your circle and starts conversing with you.
- ☐ D. Make an effort to meet new people and try to talk to people at the party who you don't know.

4. You were in a serious relationship several years ago and were completely in love. Your partner broke off the relationship and you were crushed. He or she contacts you again years later and asks to meet for lunch. You still have feelings for the person, but you are in a relationship with someone else right now. You:
   - ☐ A. Meet your ex-partner for lunch but promise yourself you will not let it go any further than that.
   - ☐ B. Decline the lunch invitation because you do not trust yourself with your ex-partner.
   - ☐ C. Meet your ex-partner for lunch and let what happens happen. Your current partner doesn't ever need to know about it.

5. You have been in a long-term relationship and the last few months have been stressful and routine. You are starting to get on each other's nerves and no longer feel any joy spending time with each other. You:
   - ☐ A. Tell your partner the relationship is no longer working and you want to break it off.
   - ☐ B. Tell your partner the relationship is in trouble and something needs to change.
   - ☐ C. Try to change the relationship for the better without discussing it with your partner.

6. You have worked at your company for several years and have been known not to take very many holidays. You finally plan a long holiday, but right before you are scheduled to leave, your company has a large project that needs to be finished and it would be impossible for them to meet the deadline with you out of town. You:

   ☐ A. Cancel the trip.

   ☐ B. Stand firm and leave for holiday as scheduled.

   ☐ C. Explain that you have planned the trip for some time but would be willing to bring some work with you to help out.

7. Your boss assigns you to a new project, but you are unsure as to whether you have the right knowledge base to complete the job successfully. You:

   ☐ A. Question why you were assigned the job in the first place.

   ☐ B. Try to bluff it and hope nobody notices.

   ☐ C. Seek out people who are more knowledgeable on the subject and ask for their help.

8. You recently changed jobs and one of your old co-workers calls you on the telephone and asks you out on a date. He/she is aware that you are not in a relationship at the moment. You enjoyed his/her conversations but you have no attraction to this person. You:

   ☐ A. Refuse outright.

   ☐ B. Gently say no, so as not to hurt the person's feelings.

   ☐ C. Try to change the subject or say you're really busy the next few weeks but you might end up going out with him/her if he/she persists.

   ☐ D. Say yes to the date even though you don't care for your ex co-worker, because it would be rude to refuse.

9. It is Friday afternoon and a few of your co-workers are planning on going out after work and you are really interested in joining them. A few suggestions on places to go are put forth, and after a co-worker suggests a specific place, everyone agrees. You do not like this place at all, however. You:

☐ A. Say nothing.

☐ B. Strenuously veto the idea.

☐ C. Mention that you don't like that place and see if they are open to going somewhere else.

10. You are a sales representative and one of your customers calls you on the phone. He is quite upset and verbal. When he tells you the problem, you realize the mistake is actually his fault. You:

☐ A. Say nothing and let him continue to talk.

☐ B. Tell him that the problem was all his fault.

☐ C. Sympathize with his situation, explain what happened, and how to correct the problem.

11. You are the manager and you ask one of your employees to do some work on a project for you. The employee returns the work to you and it is done incorrectly. You:

☐ A. Don't say anything and fix the problems yourself.

☐ B. Say the job wasn't done correctly and that it must be done again.

☐ C. Show your employee which parts of it were done correctly and those which need to be fixed.

12. You are taking clients out to a business lunch to discuss a proposal. The clients have a very small budget and you don't feel that they are worth spending much time on. Your food hasn't arrived in quite some time and you cannot find your server. A different server walks by your table and you ask him where your food is. The server

says, "I'm not your server, it's not my problem." You respond:

☐ A. I want to talk to your boss right now.

☐ B. You must be having a rough day today.

☐ C. That's not how you speak to customers.

☐ D. I know, but we're in a hurry. Please find him and send him over.

☐ E. I know you're busy too. If you happen to see him, could you ask him to come over?

13. At work, one of your co-workers has quit. You would like to apply for his position so you:

☐ A. Do nothing until the company posts the position on its website.

☐ B. Immediately confront your boss and ask for the position.

☐ C. Send your boss an email asking to set up a meeting to discuss the position.

14. You are waiting in line at the grocer's and a person cuts in front of you. You:

☐ A. Do nothing.

☐ B. Say that you were there first and the other person should get to the back of the queue.

☐ C. Clear your throat to show your displeasure.

15. You are a shift manager at the local plant. One of your employees has asked to leave early because of a personal problem. This particular employee has a history of leaving early. You:

☐ A. Let him leave early.

☐ B. Refuse because it has been happening too often lately.

☐ C. Explain that he has been leaving early much more frequently than other employees and that you need to be able to rely on him as well.

16. You are visiting various stores to do comparison shopping for a new television. At one of the stores an enthusiastic salesperson is pushing really hard for you to buy their television. You are not quite ready to make a purchase yet. You:

☐ A. Buy the television set, with the intention of returning it later if you find something better.

☐ B. Tell the salesperson to stop bothering you and walk out of the store.

☐ C. Explain that you are not ready to make a purchase yet.

17. You recently bought a new computer and are having trouble getting it to work properly so you contact the computer manufacturer's technical support line. Once on the phone, the tech support assistant is patronizing you for your lack of technical knowledge. You:

☐ A. Say nothing.

☐ B. Tell him he's being rude and demand to speak with his manager.

☐ C. Interrupt him and explain that while many people are computer savvy you are not very familiar with computers.

18. A good friend of yours starts criticizing you. You:

☐ A. Say nothing for fear of losing a friend.

☐ B. Take the opportunity to criticize him as well.

☐ C. Discuss how you feel but back off if it looks like you will start an argument.

19. You are on a date and are talking about yourself. It appears that your date isn't listening to what you are saying, so you:

☐ A. Stop talking.

☐ B. Start talking louder to get his or her attention.

☐ C. Mention to him or her that he or she appears to be distracted.

20. You return home from work and your spouse asks if you want to go out for the evening, but you would rather stay in. You:

☐ A. Go out without mentioning you'd rather stay home.

☐ B. Tell your spouse you want to be alone.

☐ C. Tell your spouse you'd rather stay home and explain why you feel this way.

21. When you are having dinner with your family you:

☐ A. Usually just listen.

☐ B. Always like to control the conversation.

☐ C. Participate in the conversation when you feel you have something valuable to add.

22. Your child asks you for an expensive toy. You cannot afford it and your child already has many toys that he does not use. You:

☐ A. Buy him the toy anyway so he won't get angry with you.

☐ B. Buy the toy, then try and return it to the store in a few weeks and hope he doesn't notice.

☐ C. Explain to him that you cannot afford the toy and that he should try and get by with the ones he already has.

23. It's wintertime and very cold outside. You are entertaining friends at your home and one of your friends decides to start smoking. You, as a non-smoker:

☐ A. Let him smoke, and open a window afterwards.

☐ B. Tell him to put the cigarette out.

☐ C. Politely tell him that you are a non-smoker and would prefer he smoke outside.

24. You have been working at your company for ten years and have not had a history of leaving work early. You have a doctor's appointment that requires you to leave work a half-hour earlier than scheduled. Instead of letting your boss know you have to leave early, you decide to leave unnoticed and hope nobody sees you. Your boss finds out you left early and the next day he comes into your office and asks what happened. You respond:

- ☐ A. I'm sorry, it won't happen again.
- ☐ B. It couldn't be helped.
- ☐ C. I understand you're upset, but I had a personal issue to attend to.
- ☐ D. Look, I never leave early, will you stop bothering me.
- ☐ E. I had an appointment that couldn't be missed, I'm sorry for not telling you.

25. Your neighbour knocks on your door and in a stern voice says to you, "Your stupid dog has been digging in my garden." You respond by saying:

- ☐ A. You don't have the right to talk to me this way.
- ☐ B. I'll keep a better eye on him. I'm sorry.
- ☐ C. He's just a dog, not a human. Relax.
- ☐ D. You look after your pets and I'll take care of mine.
- ☐ E. These things happen with pets.

26. If a friend is overdue in returning borrowed items, you:

- ☐ A. End the friendship.
- ☐ B. Give your friend the cold shoulder until he returns the borrowed items.
- ☐ C. Mention the borrowed items to your friend and ask him to return them to you.

Answer key

						Score
1.	**A** 0 points	**B** 3 points	**C** 3 points	**D** 0 points		
2.	**A** 0 points	**B** 2 points	**C** 2 points	**D** 0 points		
3.	**A** 0 points	**B** 1 point	**C** 2 points	**D** 3 points		
4.	**A** 2 points	**B** 1 point	**C** 0 points			
5.	**A** 1 point	**B** 2 points	**C** 1 point			
6.	**A** 0 points	**B** 0 points	**C** 2 points			
7.	**A** 0 points	**B** 1 points	**C** 3 points			
8.	**A** 1 point	**B** 3 points	**C** 0 points	**D** 0 points		
9.	**A** 1 point	**B** 0 points	**C** 3 points			
10.	**A** 0 points	**B** 0 points	**C** 3 points			
11.	**A** 0 points	**B** 0 points	**C** 3 points			
12.	**A** 0 points	**B** 1 point	**C** 0 points	**D** 1 point	**C** 3 points	
13.	**A** 1 point	**B** 1 point	**C** 3 points			

						Score
14.	**A** 1 point	**B** 1 point	**C** 2 points			
15.	**A** 0 points	**B** 1 point	**C** 3 points			
16.	**A** 0 points	**B** 0 points	**C** 3 points			
17.	**A** 1 point	**B** 1 point	**C** 3 points			
18.	**A** 0 points	**B** 0 points	**C** 2 points			
19.	**A** 1 point	**B** 0 points	**C** 3 points			
20.	**A** 1 point	**B** 0 points	**C** 2 points			
21.	**A** 1 point	**B** 0 points	**C** 2 points			
22.	**A** 1 point	**B** 0 points	**C** 3 points			
23.	**A** 0 points	**B** 1 point	**C** 3 points			
24.	**A** 2 points	**B** 0 points	**C** 2 points	**D** 0 points	**E** 3 points	
25.	**A** 0 points	**B** 3 points	**C** 0 points	**D** 0 points	**C** 1 point	
26.	**A** 0 points	**B** 0 points	**C** 3 points			

Determining your level of emotional intelligence

Now that you have your raw score, simply double it and this will be your Emotional Intelligence Quotient, or EQ. The range is from 0–140.

Below you will find a bell curve graph with a range of EQ scores on the bottom and a brief description of each level. The percentages in the curve represent the rarity of such a score in the general population. For example, a score of 115 will put you in the top 2 per cent of the population.

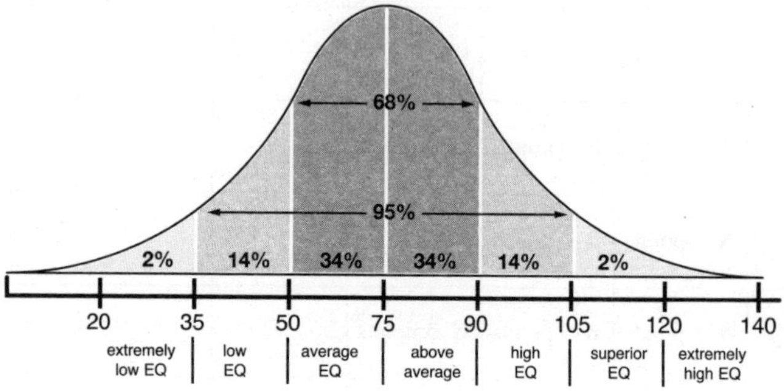

Further reading

Emotional Intelligence: Why It Can Matter More Than IQ by Daniel Goleman

Raising Your Emotional Intelligence: A Practical Guide by Jeanne Segal

3

MULTIPLE INTELLIGENCES TEST

Multiple intelligences

Eschewing traditional measures of intelligence for an intuitive approach, Howard Gardner revolutionized the field of intelligence theory with the publication of *Frames of Mind* in 1983. At first positing seven distinct intelligences – and distinguishing them from mere "talents" or "abilities" – Dr. Gardner's theories have been most robust in American education. Leaders within education instituted entire schools based on Gardner's theories. Less applicable in the workplace thus far, MI theory is solidly grounded in its applications to one's job search and success within one's chosen field.

Multiple Intelligences asks not how smart you *are* (or can be) but how smart you *act*. This is a reversal of decades of inquiry. MI theory is an interaction between eight distinct yet interrelated categories. Each of us is intelligent in the real world with some regularity depending on context and environment; consider yourself in your workplace for this exercise, interacting with colleagues, proposing a new idea to your supervisor, solving problems between yourself and co-workers who do not share your vision. While scoring highly within a particular intelligence may guide your choice of activity or vocation, one must move beyond simple self-labelling as, for example, "musically intelligent"; while the intelligences are distinct it is likely that more than one intelligence is utilized in most careers. Shunning pigeonholing into categories, the intelligent person will actively develop many intelligences at once regardless of vocation or context.

Proponents of MI theory argue that each intelligence is based on neuroimaging techniques that isolate distinct brain activity while engaged in specific activities. One's environment, ranging from one's workplace to the country in which one resides, may have a significant impact on the intelligences developed within each respective milieu. Interestingly, much research that contributed to MI theory has resulted from studies of persons with localized brain damage that negated the victim's ability to perform complete tasks within a specific intelligence.

Based on studies that isolate different parts of the brain engaged with diverse activities, people may be biologically wired to excel in one or more areas. The ability of a person to harness these intelligences and apply them is preceded by the need to "know thyself" – another method of asking the reader to develop intrapersonal intelligence. As an evolving theory, several ideas have been considered for possible inclusion in the overall definition including Digital Intelligence, Spiritual Intelligence and, yes, Sexual Intelligence. The following summaries help explain, in brief form, the eight current intelligences posited by Dr. Gardner.

1. Linguistic intelligence

Linguistic intelligence involves the use of language to facilitate understanding through the spoken word or written word. Intelligent persons exhibiting linguistic intelligence typically have an easier time mastering the demands of a scholastic environment and thrive in settings in which they can achieve success writing papers, proposals, or authoring employment manuals. Your human resources manuals might have been developed by those with intact linguistic intelligence. Conversely, one with a high level of linguistic intelligence may find him- or herself ostracized for appearing arrogant or snobbish, using "big" words that normally do not enter into everyday discourse. Once understood and embraced, the linguistically intelligent person may find an environment in which his or her talents can blossom and, ultimately, improve the working conditions for himself and those around him.

The linguistically intelligent person is keenly aware of subtleties of language. This is an asset for those in professions in which success is defined by the ability to manipulate language advantageously. Lawyers very often scale the heights of success when reviewing briefs, twisting words to benefit an argument. Doctors need high levels of linguistic intelligence to absorb voluminous amounts of information and integrate this into practice with patients. Well written emails – in contrast to quickly deteriorating standards for Internet communication – may be the *sine qua non* for those who embrace high standards in any linguistic communications.

Commonly misperceived as being "talkative", the linguistically intelligent person is able to convey richness of ideas with a minimum of words. A large vocabulary is also typically the hallmark of the linguistically intelligent person.

Leisure time spent with crosswords, anagrams, and the like may often be enjoyable for the linguistically intelligent person. One may keep a detailed journal or, in the age of the Internet, write an online blog or interact with other like-minded individuals on a public forum board.

2. Musical intelligence

Musical intelligence encompasses the ability to derive significant intellectual enjoyment from sound. This may manifest itself in the form of production, discrimination, composition, or aural entertainment. Not limited to the enjoyment of music that simply wafts from a co-worker's radio, the musically intelligent person is readily absorbed by subtleties in sound, pitch, harmony, and timbre. In fact, the musically intelligent person may not benefit from the so-called "Mozart Effect" because of its ability to absorb and distract him or her from the task at hand. Musically intelligent people may use their talents in a number of vocations not commonly associated with musical talent: a teacher may pace lectures in a way that subtly mimics the beat of a song, thus calming students, or a secretary might pace him- or herself working against the progression of a song in the background.

Naturally, the musically intelligent person will pursue musical arts with great vigour away from the workplace. Very often musically intelligent people find new methods to listen to tunes or songs heard before, might follow different paths in the musical composition, or "play with" the notes if producing them on an instrument. Enjoyment of music can be pursued with equal enjoyment individually or with others.

3. Logical-mathematical intelligence

The ability to see abstract images and work towards final goals in a stepwise manner summarizes this intelligence.

These skills are the baseline for most Western education and, like linguistic intelligence, yield high levels of success for those in educational pursuits. In the workplace, employees who have these skills are highly prized in many different fields. Typically consigned to fields such as law and architecture, the ability to formulate a coherent argument and present it to others is valued in almost any situation. The ability to convey such information necessitates high levels of linguistic intelligence as well. One without the other may lead the person to a discrete field that minimizes the less developed of the two intelligences.

Logical-mathematical intelligence is highly prized in scientific pursuits. The ability to conceptualize a theory, enumerate steps to test it, and follow through in logical progression is a natural way in which to display these skills.

4. Spatial intelligence

Those with high levels of spatial intelligence will transform visual images into concrete products for others to see. Individuals may never get lost having been to a place several years previously. City dwellers will have a natural feel for the direction in which they must go out of a train station and hikers will sense the correct path to pursue based on a quick glance at a map. Spatially intelligent people will synthesize multiple ideas into a unifying principle that crystallizes seemingly distinct concepts. Gender differences within this intelligence are most pronounced, males achieving higher levels than females, but researchers are training females to score equally on measures of mental rotation to eliminate the gender gap. Typical vocations include engineers and architects. Again, this intelligence may be highly prized and unique in vocations in which diverse people need unifying constructs. Compellingly, the ability to visualize does not require one to engage sight *per se* and, thus, people suffering from blindness can have high levels of spatial intelligence. Many people strong in this area will refer to themselves as “right-brained”, a term based in neuropsychological fact given the contribution of the right brain to these perceptions.

5. Interpersonal intelligence

People with high levels of interpersonal intelligence exhibit high levels of leadership, influence over others, and extra-version. Natural masters of group dynamics, interpersonally intelligent people are charismatic, likeable, and sought out by others in social arenas. In the workforce they often provide counsel to others, explain difficult concepts with ease, and may be better at convincing others of their positions than those with lower levels. Frequently, interpersonally intelligent people will thrive in careers in which success is based on sound sales techniques. Conversely, those who sense the needs and desires of others may also be successful within the helping professions, for example, as psychologists, clergy, or social workers.

It is common for interpersonally intelligent people to derive pleasure from frequent contact with others. These individuals may spend their off-hours with a wide range of people outside the workplace.

6. Intrapersonal intelligence

Rich awareness of one's feelings, goals, and motivations is the hallmark of the intrapersonally intelligent person. Elicited in a variety of workplace settings, those who score highly within this intelligence may be best suited for professions requiring work with others. Combined with awareness for those who are less fortunate, these people are ideally suited for charitable work as a vocation or hobby. Understanding one's emotions is not limited to those solely with a heavy heart – accountants, and engineers alike must possess the knowledge of their own abilities as well in order to effectively negotiate their immediate environs.

7. Bodily-kinesthetic intelligence

Bodily-kinesthetic intelligence is the ability to use parts of the body to solve problems or create tangible products. Traditionally conceptualized as sporting prowess, this ability also encompasses a surgeon's touch, exceptionally fast and accurate typing skill, and an artist's delicate application of paint to a canvas. Thus, gross and fine motor skills are equally weighted in this intelligence. Also notable are an actor's recreation of a famous person's gestures, a dancer's rendition of cultural expressions, and martial arts practitioners. Mentally, high achievers of bodily-kinesthetic intelligence reflexively plan physical actions with little forethought, yet can carry out actions while driving towards a goal.

8. Naturalist intelligence

This has recently been added to the growing list of intelligences. The person with high levels of naturalist intelligence will exhibit a profound ability to classify, identify patterns, and catalogue. It is primarily used to describe those who enjoy outdoor activities. These abilities also have profound implications for a corporate climate in which organizational skills are highly valued. Because of the myriad species of animals, galactic bodies and so on, the natural sciences are, so to speak, the natural vocation of the person scoring highest within this intelligence. As Stephen Jay Gould noted, Charles Darwin's major contribution to natural sciences – making order of a disparate animal kingdom – might best be classified as Gardner's naturalist intelligence. Leisure time might be spent categorizing book collections for sale on eBay, determining differences between birds while birdwatching, or engaging in deep thought while strolling through a park or walking along a hiking trail.

Given these synopses, take the Multiple Intelligences Vocational Test to determine your strengths and weaknesses.

How to take the test

The Multiple Intelligences Vocational Test comprises 79 questions. Simply indicate "true" or "false" for each statement. There is no time limit.

BEGIN TEST

1. I own a large collection of books.
   True ☐ False ☐

2. I enjoy playing with words and puns.
   True ☐ False ☐

3. Word games such as Scrabble are fun.
   True ☐ False ☐

4. I preferred school subjects such as English and social studies to maths or science.
   True ☐ False ☐

5. I enjoy a good debate about daily news items.
   True ☐ False ☐

6. I am critical of grammatical errors in others' writing.
   True ☐ False ☐

7. I have a voluminous vocabulary and seek to augment it with further study.
   True ☐ False ☐

8. I like to impress people with my erudition.
   True ☐ False ☐

9. I would enjoy writing a grant proposal or other lengthy essay to achieve a goal.
   True ☐ False ☐

10. I love to read.
    True ☐ False ☐

11. Poetry is highly rewarding when reading or writing it.
    True ☐ False ☐

12. I can fluently speak more than one language.
    True ☐ False ☐

13. I have received compliments from supervisors regarding the quality of my writing or speaking efforts.
True ☐ False ☐

14. I love to listen to music.
True ☐ False ☐

15. I can hear the same song in different ways even after I've heard it many times.
True ☐ False ☐

16. I enjoy playing a musical instrument by myself or with others.
True ☐ False ☐

17. Others enjoy my singing.
True ☐ False ☐

18. I am bothered when a familiar song skips or misplays due to a CD error.
True ☐ False ☐

19. I would not enjoy daily routines without music playing in the background.
True ☐ False ☐

20. Often I like to run a song through my head when there isn't music playing.
True ☐ False ☐

21. I like to write music lyrics for others.
True ☐ False ☐

22. I have performed a music piece or song in front of others.
True ☐ False ☐

23. I can keep track of time based on the musical selection.
True ☐ False ☐

24. Listening to music is an activity best performed while concentrating on nothing else.
True ☐ False ☐

25. I grapple with the existence of abstract concepts.
True ☐ False ☐

26. I enjoyed maths or science when at school.
True ☐ False ☐

27. I like to argue with others about facts and ideas.
True ☐ False ☐

28. I am good at organizing my living area.
True ☐ False ☐

29. I like to make sense of everything.
True ☐ False ☐

30. I enjoy mazes and jigsaw puzzles.
True ☐ False ☐

31. I am facile with mathematical equations and their applications.
True ☐ False ☐

32. When giving instructions to others, I proceed in a step-by-step procedure.
True ☐ False ☐

33. I know my way around an area after I have been there once or twice.
True ☐ False ☐

34. I am good at explaining mental images to other people.
True ☐ False ☐

35. I often have detailed, vivid dreams.
True ☐ False ☐

36. I performed better in geometry than algebra.
True ☐ False ☐

37. I can imagine myself standing somewhere else and seeing objects or people from that perspective.
True ☐ False ☐

38. I learn better when I can visualize the concepts or ideas being taught.
True ☐ False ☐

39. When someone else is speaking I can create visual images of the content.
True ☐ False ☐

40. I frequently doodle or draw as a method of maintaining concentration.
True ☐ False ☐

41. I daydream a lot.
True ☐ False ☐

42. I learn best in study groups with others.
True ☐ False ☐

43. I think of myself as a "people person".
True ☐ False ☐

44. I feel lonely when no one else is around.
True ☐ False ☐

45. Given the right circumstances, I am an effective leader of others.
True ☐ False ☐

46. I love to make others laugh.
True ☐ False ☐

47. I have a very large group of friends.
True ☐ False ☐

48. I can sense what others are thinking or feeling.
True ☐ False ☐

49. I like to help others.
True ☐ False ☐

50. I like to be the centre of attention.
True ☐ False ☐

51. I am sensitive to others.
True ☐ False ☐

52. I have high self-esteem.
True ☐ False ☐

53. I set realistic goals for myself.
True ☐ False ☐

54. I know when I am getting angry and express myself with tact.
True ☐ False ☐

55. Meditation or prayer is a part of my life.
True ☐ False ☐

56. I do my best work when I am doing it by myself.
True ☐ False ☐

57. I take pride in my identity.
True ☐ False ☐

58. I frequently reflect on the past.
True ☐ False ☐

59. I would prefer to run a business than work for someone else.
True ☐ False ☐

60. Outside of work, I generally spend time with a few select people.
True ☐ False ☐

61. I regularly exercise.
True ☐ False ☐

62. I use my hands a lot while speaking to someone in person or on the phone.
True ☐ False ☐

63. I think better when I pace back and forth.
True ☐ False ☐

64. I like to get up and walk around after sitting for a brief period of time.
True ☐ False ☐

65. At some point in my life I excelled at one or more sports.
True ☐ False ☐

66. I enjoy dancing.
True ☐ False ☐

67. I am good at fixing broken electronics or items around the house.
True ☐ False ☐

68. I like playing video games.
True ☐ False ☐

69. Sometimes I do my best thinking when I am going for a walk.
True ☐ False ☐

70. People frequently compliment my handwriting.
True ☐ False ☐

71. I need to be actively involved with a task to generate ideas or solve problems.
True ☐ False ☐

72. I love taking walks outside.
True ☐ False ☐

73. I love animals and own one or more pets.
True ☐ False ☐

74. I stop to admire flowers.
True ☐ False ☐

75. I track changing weather patterns with some regularity.
True ☐ False ☐

76. I get "stir crazy" if I spend a full day inside.
True ☐ False ☐

77. I intuitively recognize patterns and similarities.
True ☐ False ☐

78. I enjoy spending time in natural history museums.
True ☐ False ☐

79. I enjoyed studying the natural sciences such as biology, chemistry, and physics.
True ☐ False ☐

How to score this test

A simple tally of "true" responses within the question categories will reveal your MI strengths and weaknesses.

Questions 1–13:
Linguistic intelligence ___/13

Questions 14–24:
Musical intelligence ___/11

Questions 25–31:
Logical/mathematical intelligence ___/7

Questions 32–40:
Spatial intelligence ___/9

Questions 41–50:
Interpersonal intelligence ___/10

Questions 51–59:
Intrapersonal intelligence ___/9

Questions 60–70:
Bodily-kinesthetic intelligence ___/11

Questions 71–79:
Naturalist intelligence ___/9

Further reading

Gardner, Howard (1983; 1993) *Frames of Mind: The theory of multiple intelligences*, New York: Basic Books.

Gardner, Howard (1989) *To Open Minds: Chinese clues to the dilemma of contemporary education*, New York: Basic Books.

Gardner, H. (1991) *The Unschooled Mind: How children think and how schools should teach*, New York: Basic Books.

Gardner, Howard (1999) *Intelligence Reframed. Multiple intelligences for the 21st century*, New York: Basic Books.

Psychometric testing

A psychometric test is a way of assessing someone's personality in a measured way. Personality can be defined as those concepts that distinguish you from other people, make you unique, and allow a comparison between individuals. Some employers use psychometric tests to help them in their recruitment process and individuals can use them to help with their career decision-making.

The two main types of psychometric tests used are personality tests and aptitude tests. We are going to focus on the personality test here, as there is a separate aptitude test in this book.

For this test, it is not advisable to read through the questions before attempting them. There is a tendency to try to choose the "correct" answer or what you think the test designer thinks is the correct answer. It is important to answer the questions honestly if you want an accurate appraisal. Keep in mind that there are no right or wrong responses; just answer intuitively.

How to take test

You are presented with three sets of words. For each word select the column that best describes you. If the word resembles you closely, select the first column. If the word only slightly resembles you, or you feel fairly neutral or impartial, select the second column. If the word doesn't describe you at all, choose the third column.

BEGIN TEST

PART 1

How well do these words describe you?	*This characteristic describes me well*	*This somewhat describes me*	*I don't share this characteristic*
Focused			
Audacious			
Undaunted			
Effervescent			
Resolute			
Steadfast			
Tenacious			
Emphatic			
Spirited			
Sure			
Vivacious			
Vigorous			
Durable			
Buoyant			
Straight			
Resilient			
Enduring			
Definite			
Solid			
Forward			
Decisive			
Firm			
Assured			
Hardy			
Tough			

PART 2

How well do these words describe you?	*This characteristic describes me well*	*This somewhat describes me*	*I don't share this characteristic*
Changeable			
Speculative			
Unpredictable			
Controversial			
Fluctuating			
Nervous			
Peaceful			
Wordly			
Unhappy			
Tentative			
Cautious			
Suspicious			
Uneven			
Unlikeable			
Cryptic			
Unsettled			
Ambivalent			
Hesistant			
Content			
Resistant			
Restless			
Excitable			
Shy			
Fidgety			
Open			

PART 3

How well do these words describe you?	*This characteristic describes me well*	*This somewhat describes me*	*I don't share this characteristic*
Respectable			
Popular			
Conscientious			
Just			
Tolerant			
Unexceptional			
Moderate			
Balanced			
Sufficient			
Adequate			
Faithful			
Reputable			
Rational			
Conforming			
General			
Punctual			
Habitual			
Impartial			
Typical			
Accurate			
Decent			
Capable			
Proper			
Tidy			
Able			

How to score this test

For part one, add up all the selections in each of the three columns.

Each time you selected the first column in part one, give yourself five points.

Each time you selected the second column in part one, give yourself two points.

Each time you selected the third column in part one, subtract one point.

For part two, add up all the selections in each of the three columns.

Each time you selected the first column in part two, subtract two points.

Each time you selected the second column in part two, give yourself no points.

Each time you selected the third column in part two, give yourself two points.

For part three, add up all the selections in each of the three columns.

Each time you selected the first column in part three, give yourself three points.

Each time you selected the second column in part three, give yourself one point.

Each time you selected the third column in part three, give yourself no points.

Add up your totals from each part of the test to give yourself a grand total.

Interpreting your score

Although your score can range from –75 to 250, most scores fall within the 0–200 range.

200–250 points
A score within this range indicates a very strong personality. You are extremely self-confident and have a great belief in your abilities. While you are likely to be very successful in life, you have to beware of over-confidence. You might tend to get frustrated if you do not achieve your goals.

100–199 points
A score within this range indicates a generally confident, balanced personality. Those falling in this range tend to be ambitious, but not overly so, and are supportive and work well with others.

Fewer than 100 points
A score of less than 100 indicates a low level of self-confidence and a natural doubt in your abilities. You may not be working to your potential and probably let others take advantage of you at times. You may need to start working on developing your confidence and figuring out the reasons why you are not self-confident and working toward eliminating those.

4

APTITUDE TEST

Aptitude test

The Aptitude Test is designed to measure your spatial abilities, reasoning, abstract reasoning, numerical and verbal strengths. Aptitude tests are frequently used by employers, secondary schools, and the military as part of their selection process.

This test is designed so that the majority of test-takers do not finish. With this test it is important to work as quickly as you can, without sacrificing accuracy.

The test comprises 40 questions and there is a time limit of 45 minutes.

BEGIN TEST

1. PAPER is to TREE as GLASS is to:

- ☐ A. Sand
- ☐ B. Window
- ☐ C. Factory
- ☐ D. Lumber
- ☐ E. Element

2. ___ is to BRAZIL as POUND is to UNITED KINGDOM.

- ☐ A. Yuan
- ☐ B. Bhat
- ☐ C. Real
- ☐ D. Peso
- ☐ E. Euro

3. CANADA is to NORTH AMERICA as EGYPT is to:

- ☐ A. Asia
- ☐ B. Africa
- ☐ C. Europe
- ☐ D. Pacific Rim
- ☐ E. Eurasia

4. LEONARDO DA VINCI is to RENAISSANCE as VOLTAIRE is to:

- ☐ A. Existentialism
- ☐ B. Reformation
- ☐ C. Romanticism
- ☐ D. Enlightenment
- ☐ E. Post-modernism

5. JAI ALAI is to ___ as BICYCLE is to VELODROME.

- ☐ A. Aztec
- ☐ B. Court
- ☐ C. Mexico
- ☐ D. Track
- ☐ E. Fronton

6. LIQUOR is to ALCOHOLISM as FOOD is to:

- ☐ A. Overindulgence
- ☐ B. Obesity
- ☐ C. Calories
- ☐ D. Candy
- ☐ E. Stomach

7. CLARINET is to WOODWIND as TRUMPET is to:

- ☐ A. Musician
- ☐ B. Brass
- ☐ C. Instrument
- ☐ D. Percussion
- ☐ E. Copper

8. SOPRANO is to CONTRALTO as ___ is to TENOR.

- ☐ A. Soubrette
- ☐ B. Music
- ☐ C. Sing
- ☐ D. Baritone
- ☐ E. Opera

9. HAND is to ____ as FOOT is to KNEE

- ☐ A. Finger
- ☐ B. Muscle
- ☐ C. Elbow
- ☐ D. Arm
- ☐ E. Thumb

10. COLUMBIA is to BOLIVIA as TUNISIA is to:

- ☐ A. South Africa
- ☐ B. Libya
- ☐ C. Uganda
- ☐ D. Mozambique
- ☐ E. Senegal

11. Can the word COMPASS be spelt using only the letters found in the word MICROPROCESSOR?

12. Can the word SKATES be spelt by using the first letters of the words in the following sentence: Should kids attempt selling egg shells?

13. If written backwards, would the number, "Fourteen thousand, seven hundred and ninety eight," be written, "Eighty nine thousand, seven hundred and fourteen?"

14. Does the following sentence make sense if the word "puff" is understood to mean the same as the word "jog"? The puffers all thought that regular puffing would one day allow them to puff all the way around the city limits.

15. If you leave the letters in the same order but rearrange the spaces in the phrase, "Carpet asks ill you're mail" can it be read as, "Carpe task silly our email?"

16. Do the words, RESERVE, SERVERS and VERSES all use the exact same letters?

17. Is the thirteenth vowel appearing in this sentence the letter e?

18. In the English alphabet, how many letters are there between the letter O and the letter V?

19. If the word PAIN is written under the word STAR and the word PACE is written under the word PAIN and the word LICK is written under the word PACE is the word SACK formed diagonally?

20. If you remove ten letters from the word INTERPLANETARY, can the word RANT be formed?

21. Is the following sentence spelt the same forwards as it is backwards?

BUST TO HOT STUB.

22. Do the vowels in the word UNCONTROVERSIAL appear in reverse alphabetical order?

23. Change the first letter of each word to form a new word, using the same letter for both words on each line, and place the new letter between the parenthesis to form a new word vertically.

BITE	( )	PEWS
BEND	( )	VENT
BUT	( )	BAT
DOTE	( )	CASE
BARS	( )	BASE

24. BUBBLES are twice as STRONG as BOBBLES. BABBLES are three times as STRONG as BUBBLES. That means:

- ☐ A. BOBBLES are six times as STRONG as BABBLES.
- ☐ B. BABBLES are eight times as STRONG as BOBBLES.
- ☐ C. BOBBLES are eight times as STRONG as BABBLES.
- ☐ D. BABBLES are six times as STRONG as BOBBLES.

25. If most Reebings are Brongs and some Reebings are Grols, the statement that some Brongs are Grols is:

- ☐ A. True
- ☐ B. False
- ☐ C. Indeterminable from data

26. BEGIN and BEGUN are:

- ☐ A. Similar
- ☐ B. Dissimilar
- ☐ C. Opposite

27. All Astronauts are Scientists and some Scientists are Mathematicians. A few Mathematicians are Professors; therefore all Professors are Scientists.

- ☐ A. True
- ☐ B. False
- ☐ C. Indeterminable from data

28. I can buy two Bs for one A and one C for one A. I have four Bs. How many Cs can I buy?

29. Do the words DECLINES, LICENSED, and SILENCED all use the exact same letters?

30.

A B C D

31.

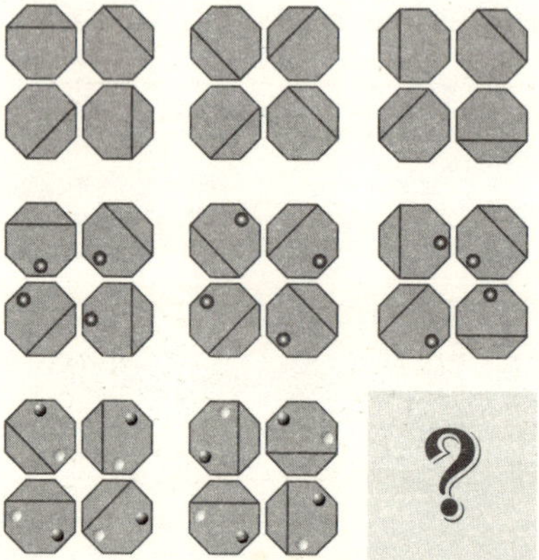

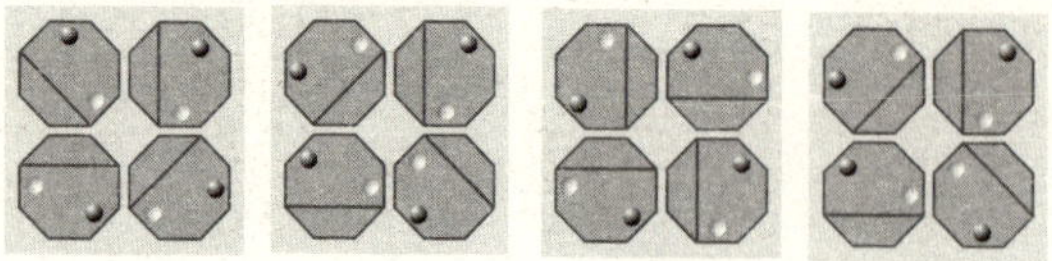

A B C D

32. Each of the six different symbols has a different value associated with it. When you add up the value of all the different symbols you get the total value for that row. The objective is to determine the value for each of the six symbols and fill in the missing value.

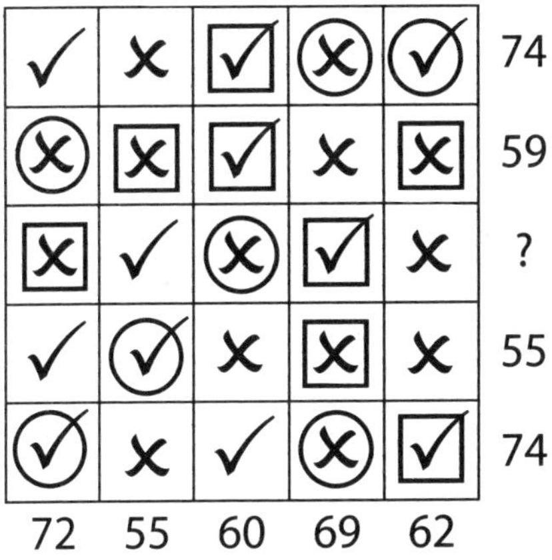

33.

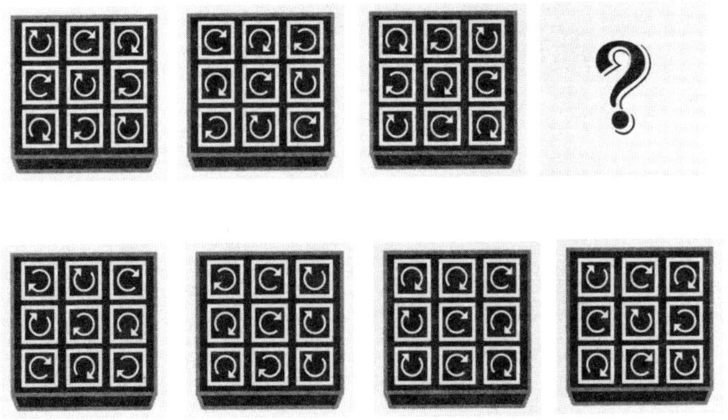

A B C D

34. Shown below is a system of wheels connected by belts. The diameter of the outer rim of each wheel is exactly twice that of the inner rim. If wheel A turns at 100 revolutions per minute, how fast will wheel E turn?

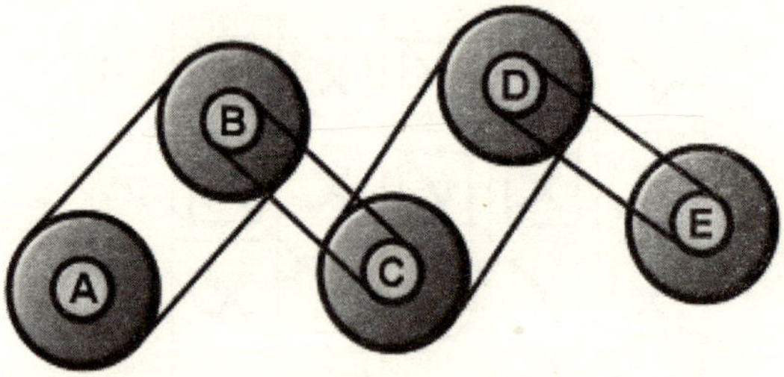

35.

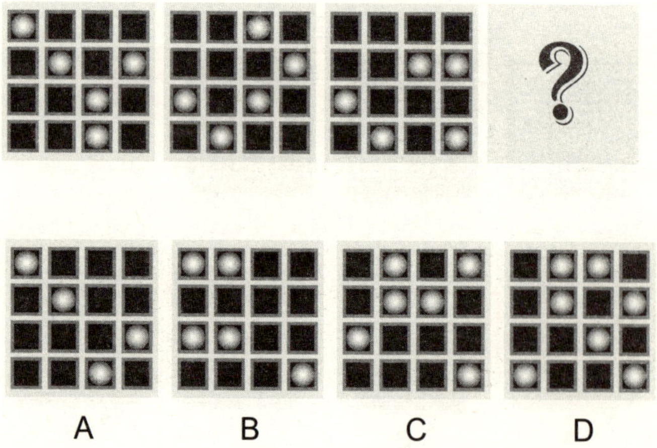

36.

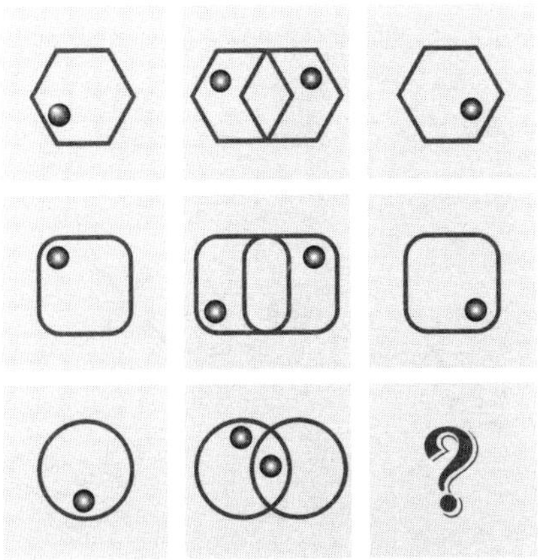

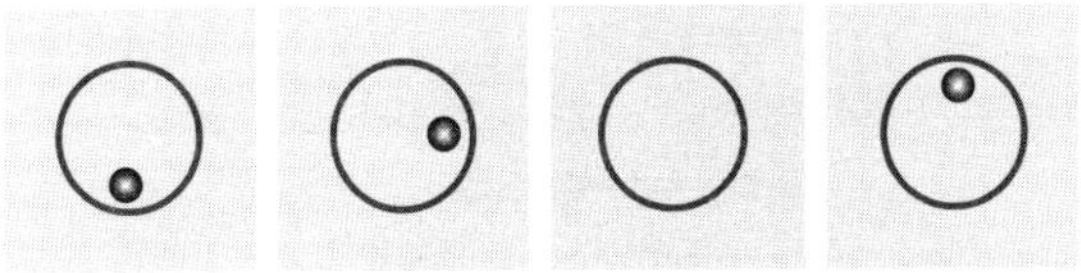

A **B** **C** **D**

37.

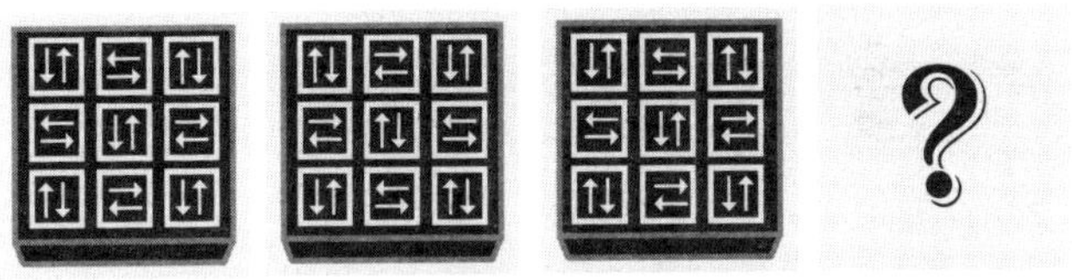

A B C D

38.

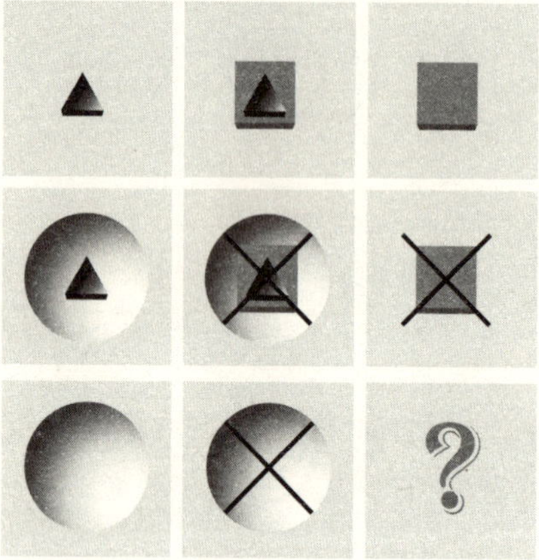

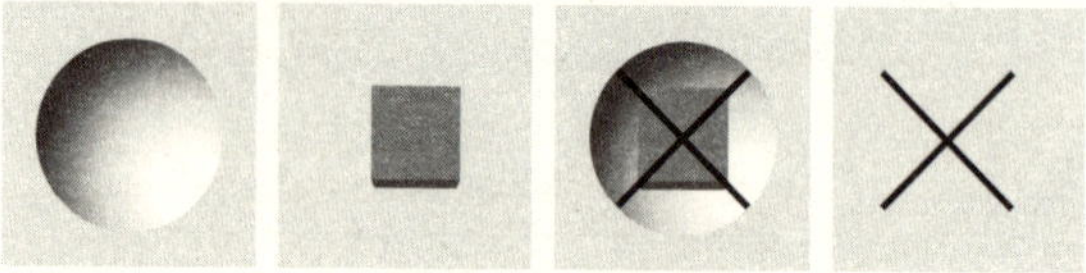

A **B** **C** **D**

39.

A B C D

40.

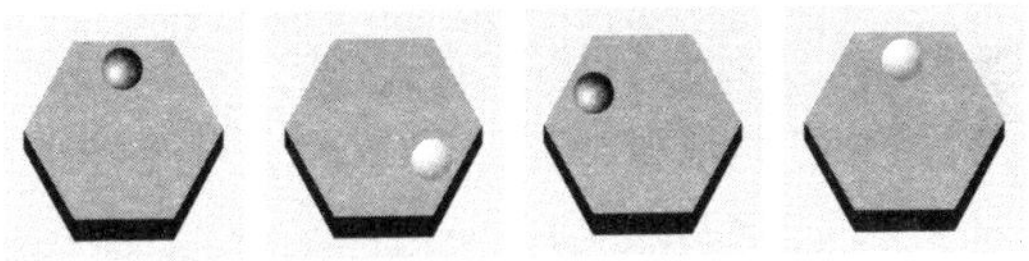

A B C D

Answer key

1. A
2. C
3. B
4. D
5. E
6. A
7. B
8. D
9. C
10. E
11. No
12. No
13. No
14. Yes
15. Yes
16. No
17. No
18. 6
19. Yes
20. Yes
21. No
22. No
23. S T O V E

SITE	(S)	SEWS
TEND	(T)	TENT
OUT	(O)	OAT
VOTE	(V)	VASE
EARS	(E)	EASE

24. D
25. C
26. A
27. C
28. 2
29. Yes
30. D
31. D
32. 56
33. D
34. 100 revolutions per minute
35. B
36. B
37. D
38. D
39. A
40. D

How to score this test

In column A locate the number of correct answers you scored on the test. In column B it will show you your approximate IQ score.

A	B
0	<70
1	70
2	72
3	74
4	76
5	78
6	80
7	82
8	84
9	86
10	88
11	90
12	92
13	94
14	96
15	98
16	100
17	102
18	104
19	106
20	108
21	110
22	112
23	114
24	116
25	118
26	120
27	122
28	124
29	126
30	128
31	130
32	132
33	134
34	136
35	138
36	140
37	142
38	144
39	146
40	150+

Further reading

The Aptitude Test Workbook by Jim Barrett

5

ASSESSING YOUR LEVEL OF ASSERTIVENESS

Assessing your level of assertiveness

This test is designed to measure three areas of interpersonal communication: passive behaviour, aggressive behaviour, and assertive behaviour.

Before we begin the test, let's discuss a bit about each of these.

Passive behaviour

Passive behaviour is characterized by letting others push you around and not standing up for your own thoughts and feelings. People with passive behaviour are typically afraid of conflict and social rejection. The passive individual frequently keeps his personal opinions, feelings and desires to himself, and can feel very frustrated and angry inside.

Some characteristics of passive behaviour are:

- Not standing up for your own rights.
- Thinking other people's needs and rights are more important than your own.
- A tendency to think that your own ideas are worthless.
- Feeling anxious about work, relationships, and family.
- Constantly apologizing for your own behaviour.
- Frequent bouts of low self-esteem.

Assertive behaviour

Assertive behaviour is characterized by a constant search for win-win solutions to social conflicts. Assertiveness involves standing up for your rights and expressing your thoughts and feelings in direct and appropriate ways. Acting assertively involves being considerate of other people's feelings without letting people take advantage of you. Possessing assertive behaviour increases the likelihood that you will get what you want without feelings of guilt.

An assertive person understands that he is naturally going to be incompatible with certain people and compatible with certain other people, and therefore, social rejection is simply an acknowledgment of social incompatibility with a given person and not a reflection of his or her worth as a person. Assertive individuals look for naturally compatible people with whom to establish relationships while avoiding naturally incompatible people.

Some characteristics of assertive behaviour are:

- Reasonable behaviour that holds its own ground and finds working compromises.
- Both sides winning at least something.
- Handling difficult situations effectively.
- Understanding which situations you can and can't handle.
- Having a sense of self-worth.
- Controlling the way you feel about the world and the people in it rather than the other way around.
- Recognizing your own and other people's rights and responsibilities.
- Always trying to be a more effective person.

Aggressive behaviour

Aggressive behaviour is characterized by a lack of concern for other people's opinions, feelings, and desires. Aggressiveness can be seen as bullying, intimidating or manipulating others, and the basic goal of aggressive behaviour is the domination of others through verbal or physical displays of power and threats of violence or retaliation. Aggressive individuals sometimes get their way in the short run, but in the long run their behaviour is self-defeating, often leaving them with few friends and many social enemies.

Unfortunately, assertiveness is often confused with aggression. People think that assertiveness means getting what you want, rather than reaching the best possible conclusion for all concerned. Aggressiveness involves standing up for your rights in a way that violates the rights of the other person, while assertiveness is concerned for both your rights and the rights of the other person.

Some characteristics of aggressive behaviour are:

- Ignoring or dismissing the needs, opinions, feelings or beliefs of others.

- Expressing your own needs, wants, opinions in inappropriate ways.

- Aggressive body language, such as shouting or acting dramatically.

- Excessive sarcasm.

- Violating the rights of others.

How to take the test

The Assertiveness Test comprises various social scenarios. To take the test, read each scenario and answer it according to your most likely reaction. There is a tendency to try to choose the "correct" answer or what you think the test designer thinks is the correct answer. It's important to answer the questions honestly if you want an accurate appraisal.

There are 18 questions and there is no time limit for this test.

BEGIN TEST

1. You are a sales representative and one of your customers calls you on the phone. He is quite upset and verbal. When he tells you the problem, you realize the mistake is actually his fault. You:

   ☐ A. Say nothing and let him continue to talk.

   ☐ B. Tell him that the problem was all his fault.

   ☐ C. Sympathize with his situation, explain what happened, and how to correct the problem.

2. You are the manager and you ask one of your employees to do some work on a project for you. The employee returns the work to you and it is done incorrectly. You:

   ☐ A. Don't say anything and fix the problems yourself.

   ☐ B. Say the job wasn't done correctly and that it must be done again.

   ☐ C. Show your employee which parts of it were done correctly and those which need to be fixed.

3. You are having dinner in a good restaurant. If your food arrives cold or the server has made a mistake with your order, you:

   ☐ A. Do nothing.

   ☐ B. Don't pay the bill.

   ☐ C. Ask the server to correct his mistake.

4. At work, one of your co-workers has quit. You would like to apply for his position so you:

   ☐ A. Do nothing until the company posts the position on its website.

   ☐ B. Immediately confront your boss and ask for the position.

☐ C. Send your boss an email asking to set up a meeting to discuss the position.

5. You are waiting in line at the grocer's and a person cuts in front of you. You:

   ☐ A. Do nothing.

   ☐ B. Say that you were there first and the other person should get to the back of the queue.

   ☐ C. Clear your throat to show your displeasure.

6. You are a shift manager at the local plant. One of your employees has asked you to leave early because of a personal problem. This particular employee has had a history of leaving early so you:

   ☐ A. Let him leave early.

   ☐ B. Refuse because it has been happening too often lately.

   ☐ C. Explain that he has been leaving early much more frequently than other employees and that you need to be able to rely on him as well.

7. You are visiting various stores to do comparison shopping for a new television. At one of the stores an enthusiastic salesperson is pushing really hard for you to buy their television. You are not quite ready to make a purchase yet. You:

   ☐ A. Buy the television set, with the intent of returning it later if you find something better.

   ☐ B. Tell the salesperson to stop bothering you and walk out of the store.

   ☐ C. Explain that you are not ready to make a purchase yet.

8. You recently bought a new computer and are having trouble getting it to work properly so you contact the computer manufacturer's technical support line. Once on the phone, the tech support assistant is patronizing you for your lack of technical knowledge. You:

- ☐ A. Say nothing.
- ☐ B. Tell him he's being rude and demand to speak with his manager.
- ☐ C. Interrupt him and explain that while many people are computer savvy you are not very familiar with computers.

9. You are going out with your friends, but they decided to do something that you have no interest in doing. You:

- ☐ A. Stay home.
- ☐ B. Demand that they change their plans and do what you want.
- ☐ C. Tell them you'd rather do something else but you'll go out with them either way.

10. A good friend of yours starts criticizing you. You:

- ☐ A. Say nothing for fear of losing a friend.
- ☐ B. Take the opportunity to criticize him as well.
- ☐ C. Discuss how you feel but back off if it looks like you will start an argument.

11. You are on a date and are talking about yourself. It appears that your date isn't listening to what you are saying, so you:

- ☐ A. Stop talking.

☐ B. Start talking louder to get his or her attention.

☐ C. Mention to him or her that he or she appears to be distracted.

12. You have worked at your company for several years and have been known not to take very many holidays. You finally plan a long holiday, but right before you are scheduled to leave, your company has a large project that needs to be finished and it would be impossible for them to meet the deadline with you out of town. You:

☐ A. Cancel the trip.

☐ B. Stand firm and leave for your holiday as scheduled.

☐ C. Explain that you have planned the trip for some time but would be willing to take some work with you to help out.

13. You return home from work and your spouse asks if you want to go out for the evening, but you would rather stay in. You:

☐ A. Go out without mentioning you'd rather stay home.

☐ B. Tell your spouse you want to be alone.

☐ C. Tell your spouse you'd rather stay home and explain why you feel this way.

14. You are at work and are attending a company meeting. Your boss asks for your opinion on a matter, but you realize your opinion may not go over well with everyone. You feel strongly about your opinion. You:

☐ A. Say that you would prefer to discuss it after the meeting in private.

- ☐ B. Just come right out and say what you think.
- ☐ C. Preface your opinion by saying that not everyone may agree before making your case.

15. If a friend is overdue in returning borrowed items, you:

- ☐ A. End the friendship.
- ☐ B. Give your friend the cold shoulder until he returns your item.
- ☐ C. You mention the borrowed items to your friend and ask him to return them to you.

16. When you are having dinner with your family you:

- ☐ A. Usually just listen.
- ☐ B. Always like to control the conversation.
- ☐ C. Participate in the conversation when you feel you have something valuable to add.

17. Your boss assigns you to a new project, but you are unsure as to whether you have the right knowledge base to complete the job successfully. You:

- ☐ A. Question why you were assigned the job in the first place.
- ☐ B. Try to bluff it and hope nobody notices.
- ☐ C. Seek out people who are more knowledgeable on the subject and ask for their help.

18. It's wintertime and very cold outside. You are entertaining friends at your home and one of your friends decides to start smoking. You, as a non-smoker:

- ☐ A. Let him smoke, and open a window afterwards.

☐ B. Tell him to put the cigarette out.

☐ C. Politely tell him that you are a non-smoker and would prefer he smoke outside.

How to score this test

There are three main types of behaviour that we are measuring here: aggressive behaviour, passive behaviour, and assertive behaviour.

Each time you answered A, record one point for passive behaviour.

Each time you answered B, record one point for aggressive behaviour.

Each time you answered C, record one point for assertive behaviour.

If the questions were answered honestly there should be a mix of all three behaviour patterns. The more points you have for any one specific behaviour, the more dominant that trait is with you. If you scored 10 or more points for a certain behaviour, it is very strong with you. At the beginning of the test we discussed what these traits entail and certain characteristics of them. Whichever was your dominant trait, go back and review the characteristics. If you answered the questions honestly, some of the characteristics listed should mirror yours.

Further reading

The Assertiveness Workbook by Randy Paterson
Assertiveness Skills by Nelda Shelton

6

ASSESSING YOUR LEADERSHIP SKILLS

Assessing your leadership skills

Let's take a moment to familiarize you with a few of the major theories of leadership.

The Great Man theory

This theory's main assumption is that leaders are born and not made and that great leaders will arise when there is a great need.

Early on, most research on leadership was conducted on people who were already great leaders. These people were often from the aristocracy, and contributed to the notion that leadership had something to do with breeding. The Great Man theory strayed from this line of thinking and suggested that, in times of need, a Great Man would arise, regardless of aristocracy or breeding.

The Trait theory

This theory's main assumption is that people are born with inherited traits and that some traits are particularly suited to leadership. People who make good leaders have the right combination of such traits. This theory sought to discover these inherited traits by studying successful leaders, but with the underlying assumption that if other people could also be found with these traits, then they too could become great leaders.

Behavioural theory

This theory's main assumption is that leaders can be made, rather than only being born and that successful leadership is based on definable, learnable behaviour.

Behavioural theory does not look for inborn traits or capabilities; rather, it looks at what leaders actually do.

Participative leadership

This theory's main assumption is that people are less competitive and more collaborative when they are working on joint goals. When people make decisions together, the social commitment to one another is greater and therefore increases their commitment to the decision. In short, several people deciding together make better decisions than one person alone. A participative leader looks to involve other people in the process rather than making autocratic decisions.

Situational leadership

This theory's main assumption is that when a decision is needed, an effective leader does not just fall into a single preferred style of leadership, but changes his strategy according to the situation.

Contingency theory

This theory's main assumption is that a leader's ability to lead is contingent upon several situational factors, including the leader's preferred style and the capabilities and behaviours of followers.

Contingency theory contends that there is no single best way of leading, and that a leadership style that is effective in some situations may not be successful in others.

For example, leaders who are very effective in one situation may become unsuccessful either when transplanted to another situation or when the factors around them change.

Transactional leadership

This theory's main assumption is that people are motivated by reward and punishment, and leadership works most effectively with a clear chain of command.

The transactional leader defines what is required of their employees and the rewards that they get for following orders. Punishments are also well understood and formal systems of discipline are usually in place

Transformational leadership

This theory's main assumption is that people will follow a person who inspires them and that a person with vision and passion can achieve great things. With this theory, the most effective way to get things done is by injecting enthusiasm and energy. Transformational leaders often use ceremonies, awards and other perks to continually motivate their employees.

Here is a list of characteristics often displayed by those with team and leadership prowess:

- Adaptable to situations.
- Alert to the social environment.
- Ambitious and achievement-orientated.
- Assertive, cooperative, decisive.
- Persistent, self-confident.
- Tolerant of stress.
- Willing to assume responsibility.
- Ability to articulate a vision.
- A willingness to assume personal risk to pursue a vision.
- Use of unconventional strategies.
- Emotional stability and composure.
- Admitting error, owning up to mistakes.

How to take the test

The Leadership Skills Test is designed to measure your leadership strengths and weaknesses, which will allow you to discover your ability to lead others to success. Like many traits, leadership can be improved with effort and self-knowledge.

It's important to judge yourself honestly when answering the questions. The more honest your answers are, the more accurate your results will be.

There are 56 questions followed by a ranking from Never to Always. After reading each question, tick the box that you feel is the most appropriate answer.

There is no time limit for this test.

BEGIN TEST

How often do you display this quality?	*Never*	*Rarely*	*On Occasion*	*Often*	*Always*
Do you have clear expectations and goals at work?					
Do you expect the best from people?					
Do you display trust in people?					
Can you direct people or projects?					
Do you have a positive outlook?					
Do you consider yourself good at delegating?					
Do you consider yourself flexible with changes?					
Do you find yourself trying to build morale in your company?					
Do you tend to embrace error and mistakes you make?					
Are you adaptable to change?					
Do you have a take-charge attitude?					
Do you give criticism constructively?					
Are you results-oriented?					
Do you communicate well, both in the spoken word, and in writing?					

How often do you display this quality?	*Never*	*Rarely*	*On Occasion*	*Often*	*Always*
Are you enthusiastic and lively?					
Do you encourage feedback and unsolicited opinions?					
Are you open to new ideas?					
Do you consider yourself supportive of others?					
Can you be persuasive?					
Do you take risks?					
Do you find yourself playing the role of adviser?					
Do you have a positive attitude?					
Are you well-spoken?					
Do you set goals for people?					
Do you consider yourself knowledgeable?					
Are you decisive?					
Are you understanding?					
Do you have a strong sense of purpose?					

How often do you display this quality?	*Never*	*Rarely*	*On Occasion*	*Often*	*Always*
Do you set priorities and goals?					
Do your employees feel you have credibility?					
Do you act as a mentor to anyone?					
Are you a problem-solver?					
Do you achieve your goals?					
Do you manage your time well?					
Do you act as a good role model to others?					
Do you consider yourself personable?					
Do you display optimism?					
Do you consider yourself a dreamer?					
Do you have good social skills?					
Do you empower other people?					
Do you spend time teaching and developing employees?					
Are you self-confident?					

How often do you display this quality?	*Never*	*Rarely*	*On Occasion*	*Often*	*Always*
Are you completely dedicated?					
Do you give technical support?					
Do you listen well to others?					
Do you enjoy going to work?					
Do you try to work on team building?					
Are you continually learning?					
Do you allow yourself to quit before you complete your work?					
Is your work completed long before it is due?					
Do people come to you with their problems?					
Do you have difficulty telling a co-worker when he/she is being troublesome?					
Are you constantly trying to change things?					
Do you enjoy speaking in front of people?					
Do you forgo your social life to complete work?					
Do you/did you pride yourself on your grades in school?					

Answer key

Use the following method for scoring this test.

For each box you checked NEVER, give yourself 2 points.

For each box you checked RARELY, give yourself 1 point.

For each box you checked ON OCCASION, give yourself 0 points.

For each box you checked OFTEN, give yourself 2 points.

For each box you checked ALWAYS, give yourself 4 points.

How to interpret your score

While the scoring spectrum ranges from 112 to 224, most scores are going to fall somewhere between 0–150.

150+	Excellent leadership skills
125–150	High level of leadership abilities
100–124	Above average leadership skills
75–99	Average leadership skills
50–74	Below average leadership skills
25–49	Indicative of passive, introverted behaviour
<25	Extremely poor leadership abilities

Further reading

Test your Leadership Skills by Brian O'Neill

7

ASSESSING YOUR WORKING MEMORY

Assessing your memory

Your working memory plays a crucial role in determining your ability to understand a spoken sentence, calculate a restaurant tip in your head, or remember a string of digits such as a phone number. Working memory is one of the most important concepts in understanding and improving your memory, and your working memory capacity is what best measures your memory intelligence. Psychology pioneers in the 1950s and 1960s developed the concept of short-term memory, which they described as the part of memory which stores a limited amount of information for a limited amount of time, usually under a minute. Working memory is a relatively recent term; a refinement of the older concept of short-term memory. It takes the idea of short-term memory and expands on it, suggesting that short-term memory is woven together with higher cognitive processes, such as learning, reasoning, and comprehension.

Over the years, working memory has been broken down into several components. A visuospatial sketchpad that holds visual and spatial information, a phonological loop for holding verbal information, the articulatory loop – or the "inner voice" – which functions as a rehearsal system for your own spoken words, and a central executive that decides what information enters, stays and is let go from the visuospatial sketchpad and phonological loop.

Different from long-term memory (often described as a library, a filing system, a storage facility), working memory contains the information which you are immediately using. In order to store information in our long-term memory, it must be "worked" in via our working memory. When retrieving information from long-term memory, we again use our working memory to "remember" something. One of the most widely known facts about working memory is that it can only hold around seven "packets" of information. Alone, this tells us little about the limits of working memory because the size of the packet isn't concrete. The United States is one of the only Western countries to cling to a seven-digit phone number system, and the number of digits was arrived upon in part by the studies done suggesting that civilians could only remember up to seven numbers in their head. The problem is, 1, 2, 3, 4, 5, 6, and 7 could be seen as seven different packets, if you remember each digit separately, or as a single packet of 1 through 7. More recently, research has suggested that it's not so much the number of chunks that is important but how long it takes you to say the words. In recent studies it appears that you can only hold in working memory what you can say in about one-and-a-half to two seconds.

How to take the test

The Working Memory Test comprises two sections: text comprehension and visuospatial working memory. For the text comprehension section, you are given a short passage to read. Read the passage once and answer the questions regarding the material.

For the visuospatial working memory section you are shown a grid with differing images in it. Take exactly 60 seconds to memorize the layout of the grid and then turn the page and try to locate the exact layout from the choices shown.

BEGIN TEST

Section 1: Text comprehension, part 1

Dogs Playing Poker is a series of paintings by Cassius Marcellus Coolidge. In 1903, the advertising firm Brown & Bigelow commissioned a series of 16 paintings from Coolidge to depict dogs acting like humans. Of these 16, nine show the dogs seated around a card table, playing poker and smoking cigars. They show various stages of what might be the same poker game; for example, in *A Bold Bluff,* a Saint Bernard's hand can be seen by the viewer but not by the other dogs. In *Waterloo*, the Saint Bernard takes his winnings. *Looks Like Four of a Kind* is a well-known painting that was a follow-on to the original series.

The series has a kitschy appeal that has made it part of American pop culture. For example, in Larry Shue's play *The Foreigner*, a character staying in a lodge remarks she does not want to be in her room because "the damned painting [in there] is *Dogs Playing Poker*".

After intense bidding, *A Bold Bluff* and *Waterloo: Two* sold to a private collector from New York City for $590,400 in 2005.

1. What was the first name of the painter?

- ☐ A. Calvin
- ☐ B. Marcellus
- ☐ C. Coolidge
- ☐ D. Cassius

2. What was the name of the advertising firm that commissioned the paintings?

- ☐ A. Branch and Williamson
- ☐ B. Barry and Wilson
- ☐ C. Brown and Bigelow
- ☐ D. Breston and Barnes

3. Of the 16 paintings commissioned, how many showed dogs seated around a card table, playing poker and smoking cigars?

- ☐ A. None
- ☐ B. 6
- ☐ C. 9
- ☐ D. 16

4. According to the article, which one was a well-known painting that was a follow-on to the original series?

- ☐ A. *Looks Like Four of a Kind*
- ☐ B. *Waterloo: Two*
- ☐ C. *A Bold Bluff*
- ☐ D. There was no mention of a follow-on painting in the article

5. In which painting could a Saint Bernard's hand can be seen by the viewer but not by the other dogs?

- ☐ A. *Looks Like Four of a Kind*
- ☐ B. *Waterloo*
- ☐ C. *A Bold Bluff*
- ☐ D. *The Foreigner*

Section 1: Text comprehension, part 2

The Spruce Goose is a nickname commonly given to the Hughes H-4 Hercules, an aircraft designed and built by the Hughes Aircraft Company. It is the largest flying boat, and has the largest wingspan of any aircraft ever built. Only one was built.

The aircraft was the brainchild of Henry J. Kaiser, who directed the Liberty Ships programme. He teamed up with aircraft designer Howard Hughes to create what would become the largest aircraft ever built or even seriously contemplated at that time. When completed, it would be capable of carrying 750 fully-equipped troops or two Sherman tanks.

Due to wartime restrictions on the availability of metals, the H-4 was built almost entirely of laminated birch, not spruce as its name suggests. The aircraft was a marvel in its time. It married a soon-to-be outdated technology – flying boats – to a massive airframe that required some truly ingenious engineering innovations.

On 2 November 1947, with Howard Hughes personally at the controls, the Spruce Goose lifted off from the waters off Long Beach, California, remaining airborne 70 feet off the water at a speed of 80 mph for just under a mile. At this altitude the plane was still in ground effect and some critics believe it was too lacking in power to truly fly.

In 1988, the Spruce Goose was acquired by The Walt Disney Company, but due to the lacklustre revenue the Spruce Goose Exhibit generated, Disney began to look for another organization to take it off its hands. After a long search for a qualified buyer, the plane was acquired by the Evergreen Aviation Museum in 1993, which disassembled the aircraft and moved it by barge to its current home in McMinnville, Oregon, where it has been on display since.

1. According to the article, what type of material was the Spruce Goose made of?

- ☐ A. Spruce
- ☐ B. Poplar
- ☐ C. Birch
- ☐ D. Balsa

2. What year did the Spruce Goose first fly?

- ☐ A. 1941
- ☐ B. 1944
- ☐ C. 1947
- ☐ D. 1976

3. What is the name of the town where the Spruce Goose is housed?

- ☐ A. Long Beach
- ☐ B. McMinnville
- ☐ C. Portland
- ☐ D. Acadia

4. According to the article why did some critics believe it was too lacking in power to truly fly?

- ☐ A. Ground effect
- ☐ B. Wingspan
- ☐ C. It could only land on water
- ☐ D. It was too heavy

5. How many troops could the Spruce Goose hold?

- ☐ A. 300
- ☐ B. 450
- ☐ C. 700
- ☐ D. 750

6. According to the article, the aircraft was the brainchild of?

- ☐ A. Howard Hughes
- ☐ B. Walt Disney
- ☐ C. Henry J. Kaiser
- ☐ D. Henry Manville

Section 2: Visuospatial working memory

For this section, you are asked to memorize the layout of the items in the diagrams below. Spend 60 seconds memorizing the layout of the images in Diagram 1 and then look at page 121 and try to locate the exact layout from the choices shown. Once you've chosen an answer, do the same with Diagram 2. There are four diagrams in all.

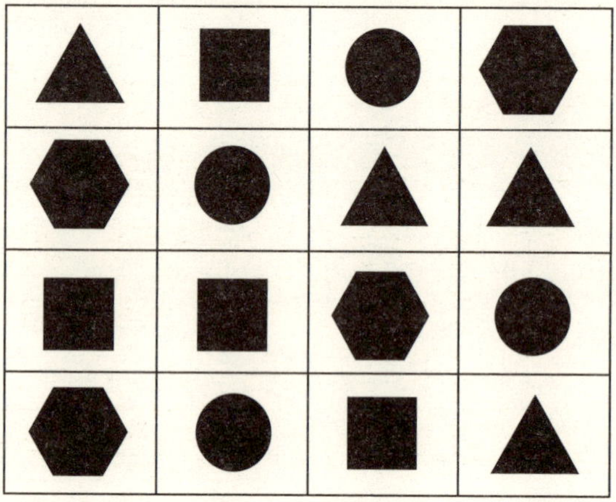

Diagram 1

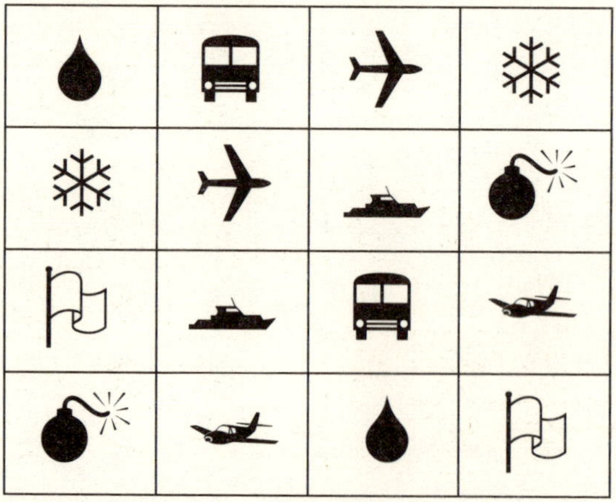

Diagram 2

Diagram 1 answers

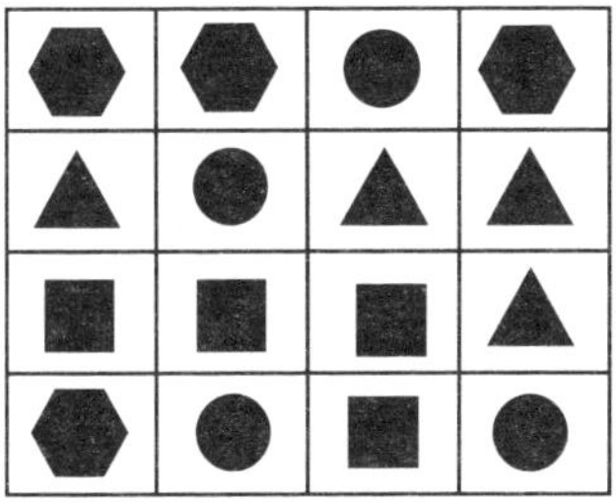

A

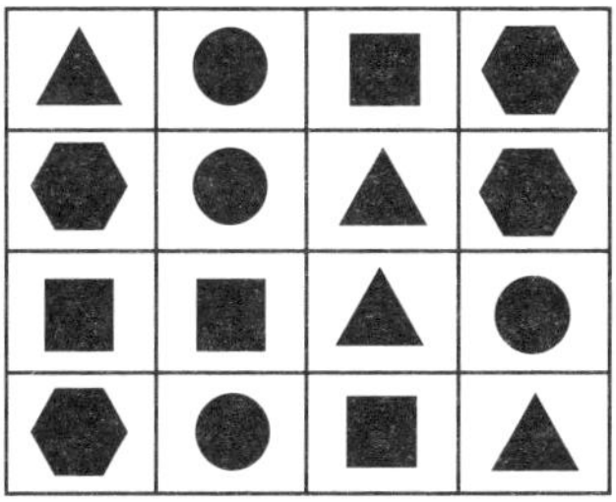

B

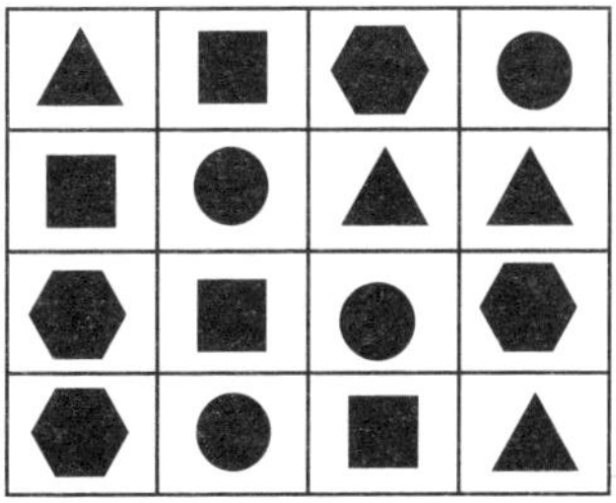

C

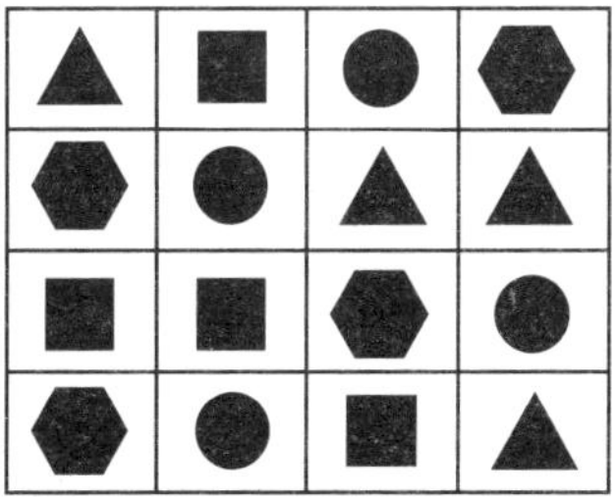

D

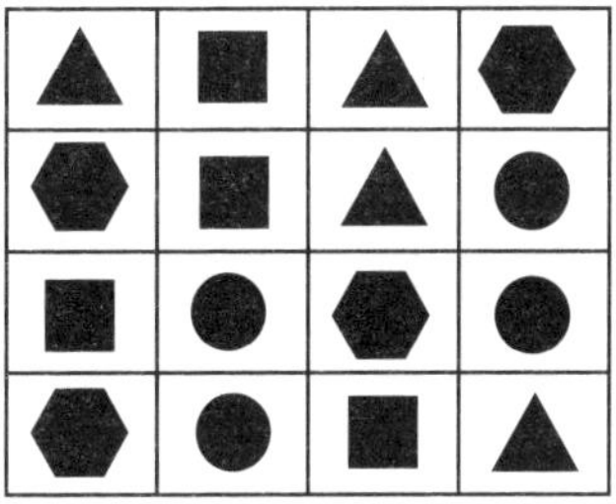

E

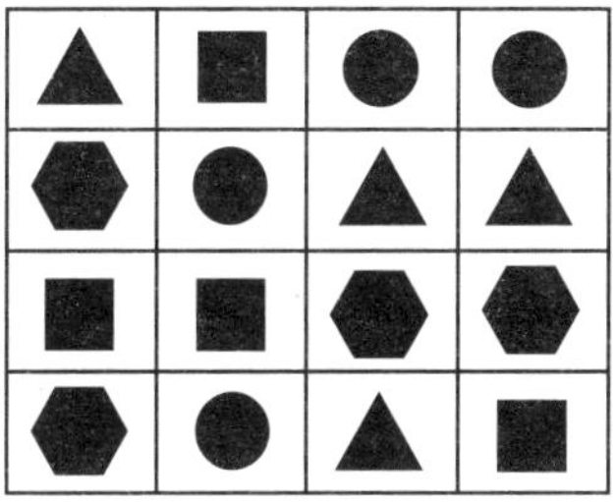

F

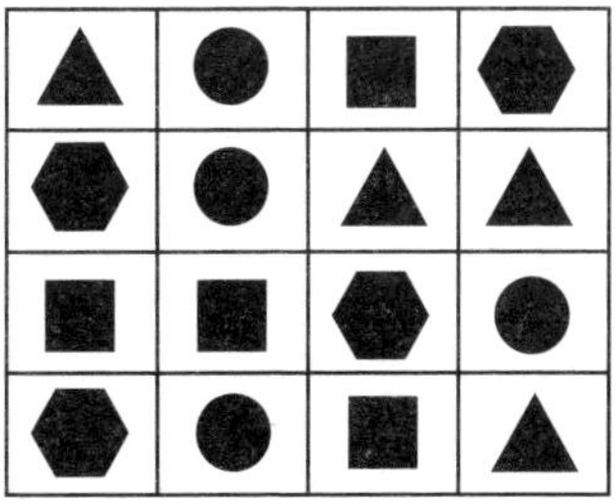

G

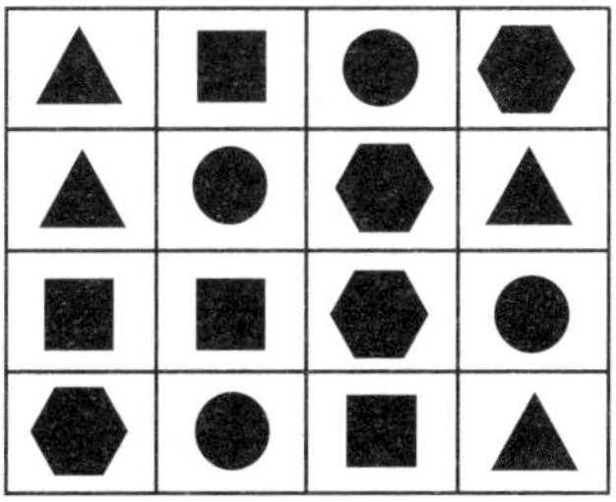

H

Diagram 2 answers

A

B

C

D

E

F

G

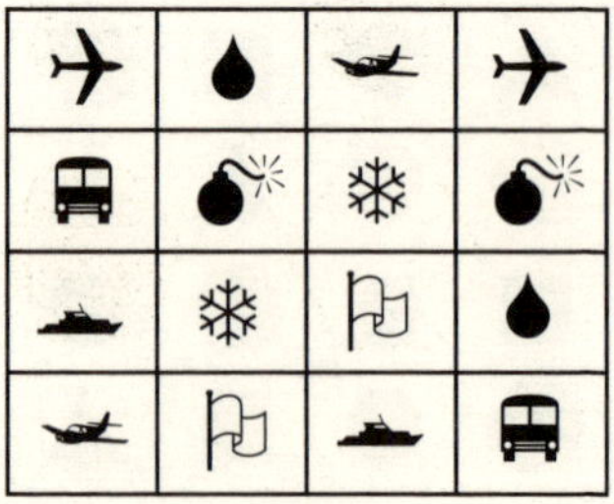

H

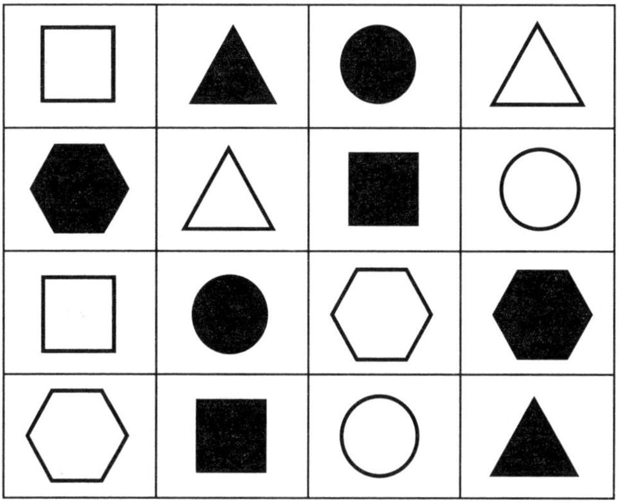

Diagram 3

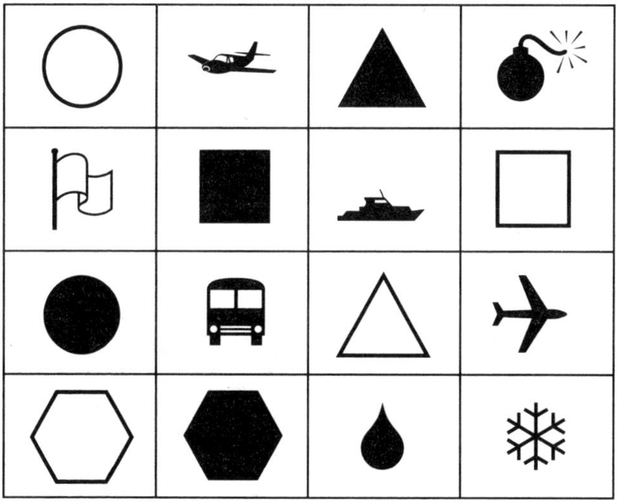

Diagram 4

Diagram 3 answers

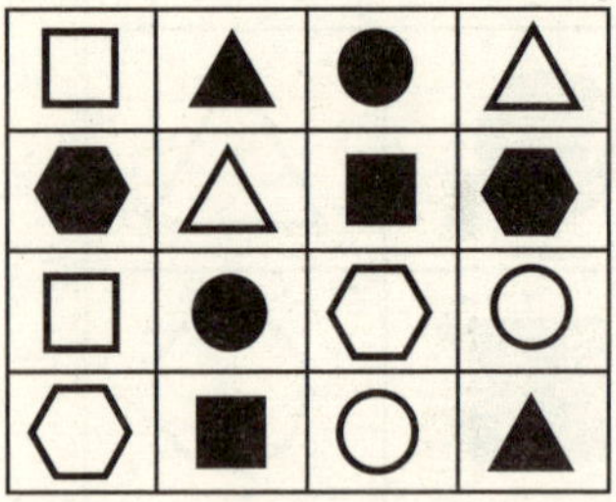

A

B

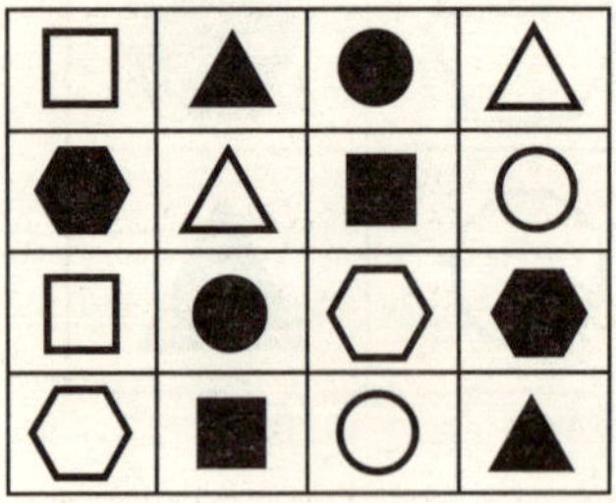

C

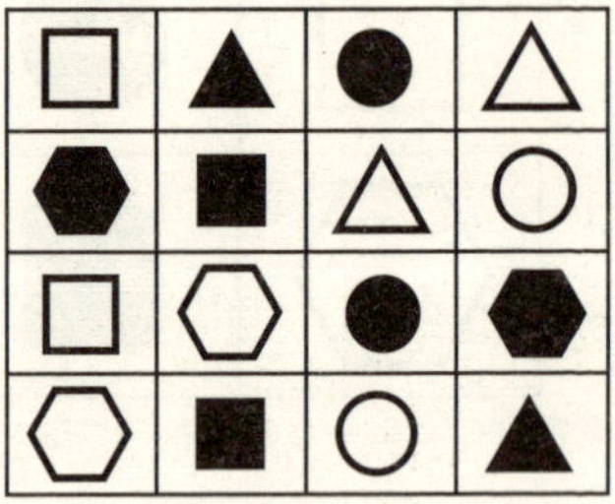

D

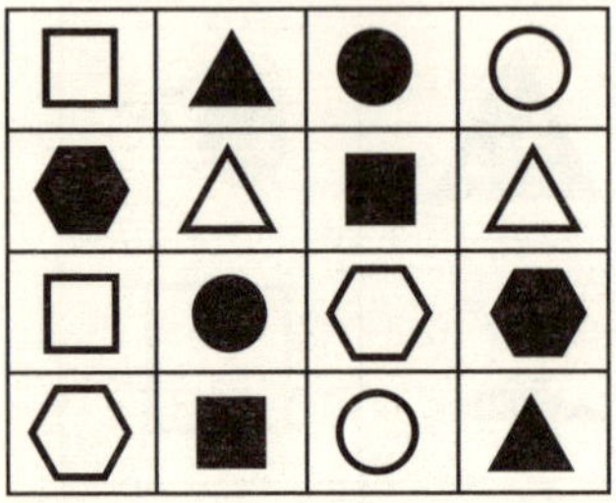

E

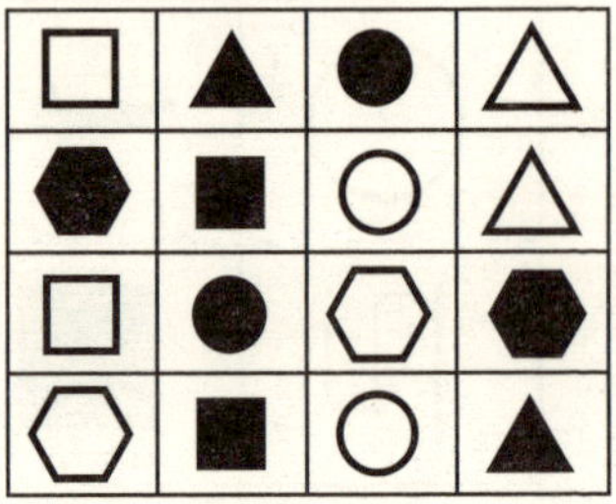

F

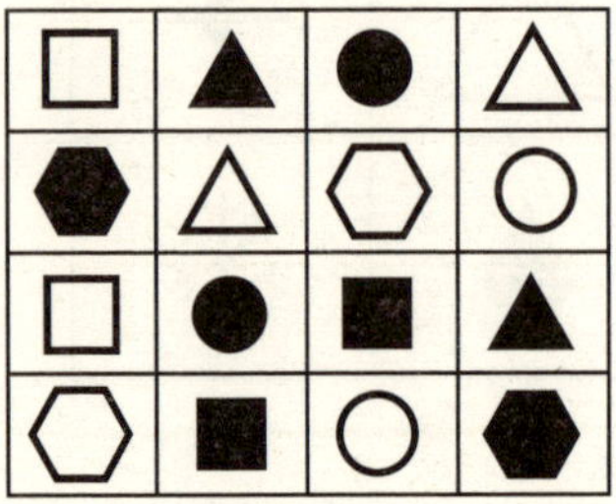

G

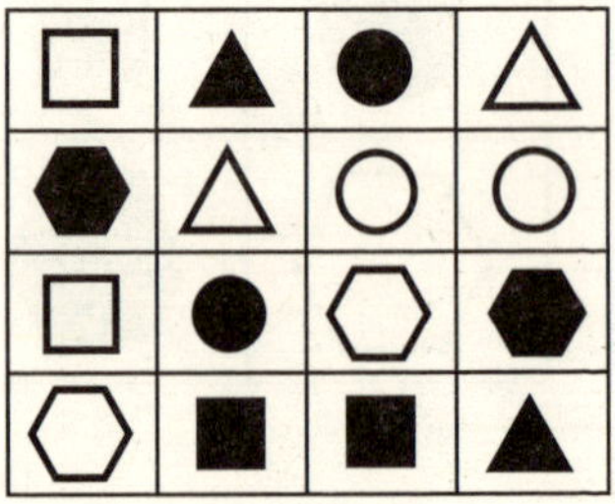

H

Diagram 4 answers

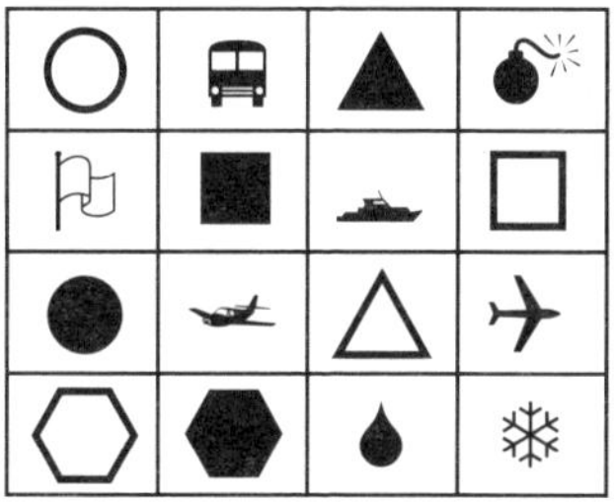

A

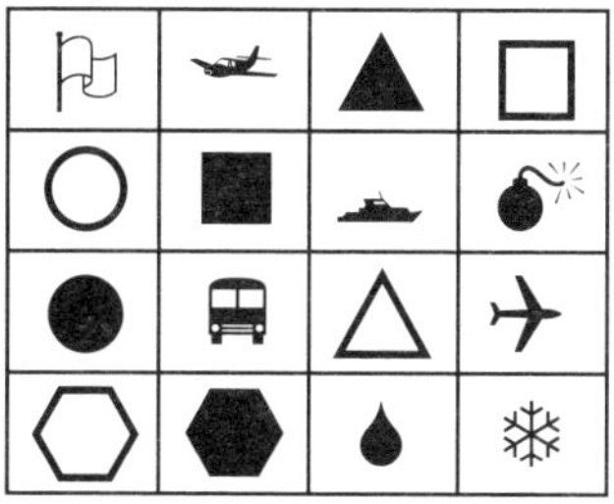

B

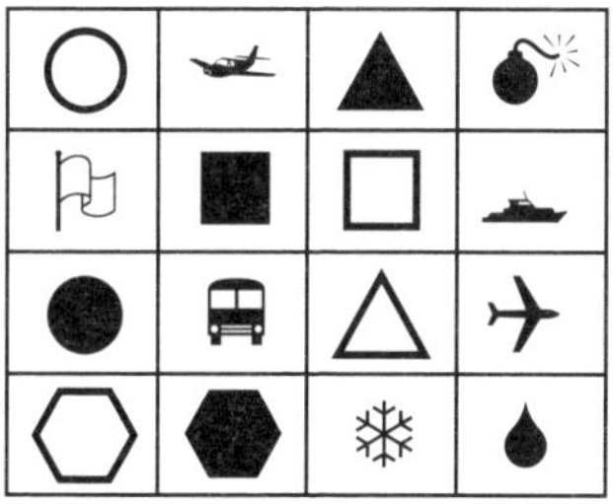

C

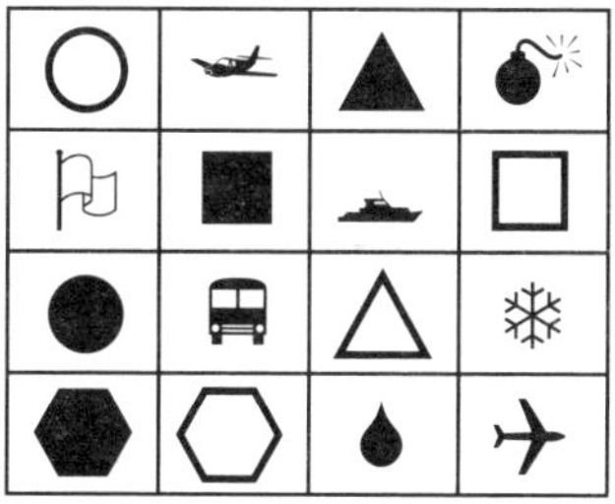

D

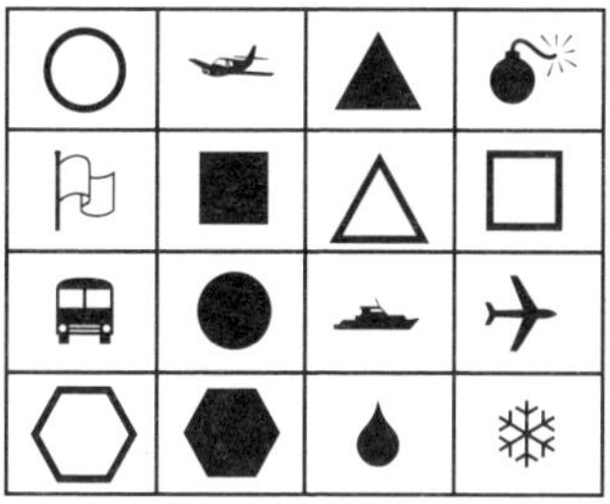

E

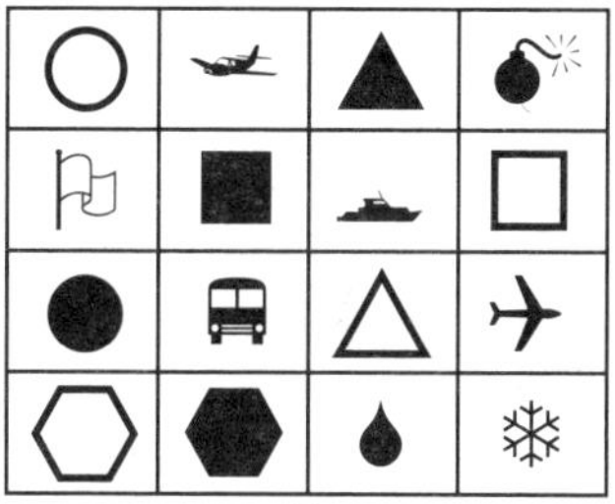

F

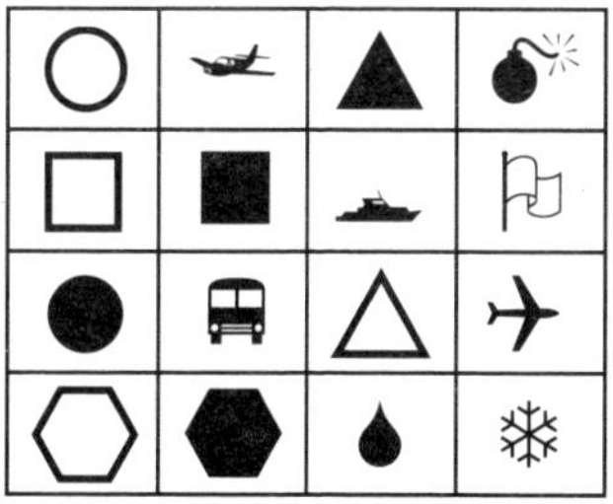

G

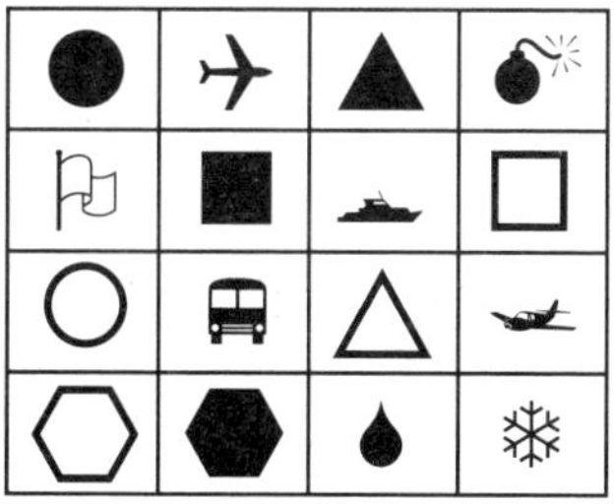

H

Answer key

Section 1: Text comprehension, part 1

1. D
2. C
3. C
4. A
5. C

Section 1: Text comprehension, part 2

1. C
2. C
3. B
4. A
5. D
6. C

Section 2: Visuospatial working memory

Memory diagram 1: D
Memory diagram 2: G
Memory diagram 3: C
Memory diagram 4: F

Interpreting your score

Below you will find a bell curve graph with a range of IQ scores on the bottom and a brief description of each level. The percentages in the curve represent the rarity of such a score in the general population. For example, a score of 115 will put you in the top 16 per cent of the population.

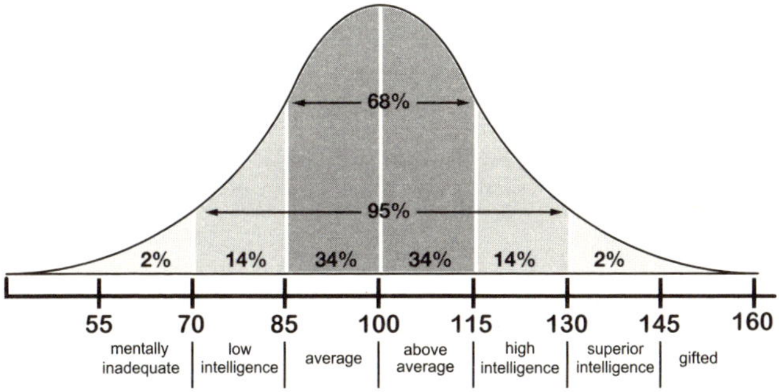

It's important to keep in mind that since this test is not given under controlled conditions, it cannot give a true IQ score. The score given on this test is intended merely as an indicator of how a person might perform on an IQ test.

Further reading

Short-Term and Working Memory by Susan Gathercole
Visuo-Spatial Working Memory by Robert H. Logie

8

ASSESSING YOUR MATHEMATICAL INTELLIGENCE

Assessing your mathematical intelligence

Mathematical intelligence is the capacity to use numbers effectively and to reason well; traditional IQ tests and achievement tests rely heavily on maths questions. Those who excel in maths tend to think conceptually in logical and numerical patterns and do well with tasks such as problem solving, handling long chains of reason to make logical progressions, and performing complex mathematical calculations.

We all require some numerical skills in our lives, whether it's to calculate a restaurant tip or to balance our chequebook. Mathematical intelligence is your ability to calculate basic arithmetic computations, and helps you to understand geometric shapes and manipulate equations. The reason it's such a strong indicator of general intelligence is because many everyday mental tasks require mathematical operations even when numbers are not involved.

Some characteristics of mathematical intelligence are:

- The ability to easily compute numbers mentally.
- Noticing and using numbers, shapes, and patterns.
- Moving from the concrete to the abstract easily.
- Exploring patterns and logical sequences and relationships.
- The belief that everything has a rational explanation.

How to take the test

There are 38 multiple-choice questions dealing with all aspects of mathematical intelligence. You have only 45 minutes to complete the test, so it's advisable not to spend too much time on any single question. The use of pencil and paper is allowed, but not of electronic devices such as calculators and computers, and your score will not be as accurate if they are used. For the most accurate score possible, it's crucial to stay within the time limit and to use only pencil and paper to solve the problems.

BEGIN TEST

1. If one apple costs 12p how much will a dozen and a half apples cost?

   - ☐ A. £1.20
   - ☐ B. £1.44
   - ☐ C. £1.92
   - ☐ D. £2.16
   - ☐ E. £2.40

2. A car dealer paid £20,000 for some used cars. He sold them for £27,500, making an average of £1,500 on each car. How many cars did he sell?

   - ☐ A. None
   - ☐ B. 1
   - ☐ C. 5
   - ☐ D. 20
   - ☐ E. 50

3. If it takes four bricklayers an hour to build a wall, how long will it take five of them to build the same wall?

   - ☐ A. 30 minutes
   - ☐ B. 45 minutes
   - ☐ C. 48 minutes
   - ☐ D. 50 minutes
   - ☐ E. 60 minutes

4. A bag of coffee beans costs £250 and contains 100 possible servings. How much must the proprietor sell a cup of coffee for to make 150 per cent profit per bag?

   - ☐ A. £2.50
   - ☐ B. £5.00
   - ☐ C. £6.25
   - ☐ D. £7.50
   - ☐ E. £10.00

5. If a pair of trousers requires one-and-a-half as much cloth as a shirt, and the total cloth used for the trousers

and the shirt costs £50, how much does the cloth for the trousers cost?

- ☐ A. £25
- ☐ B. £30
- ☐ C. £35
- ☐ D. £40
- ☐ E. £45

6. A sushi restaurant buys twenty fish for £10 each. The owner knows that 50 per cent of the fish will go bad before being served. Each fish creates 10 servings. What price must the owner charge per serving in order to make a 100 per cent profit on this initial investment?

- ☐ A. £4
- ☐ B. £6
- ☐ C. £8
- ☐ D. £10
- ☐ E. £20

7. Three partners venture on a project. They prorate their (potential) profits over their £11,000 investment. Sam invests twice as much as Peter. Peter invests 50 per cent more than Charlie. If the venture breaks even how much does Charlie get back?

- ☐ A. £1,500
- ☐ B. £2,000
- ☐ C. £2,500
- ☐ D. £5,500
- ☐ E. $11,000

8. A basketball player makes one-third of his shots from the foul line. How many shots must he take to make 100 baskets?

- ☐ A. 100
- ☐ B. 101

☐ C. 300
☐ D. 301
☐ E. 303

9. A submarine averages 10 kilometres an hour under water and 25 kilometres per hour on the surface. How many hours will it take it to make a 350 kilometre trip if it goes two-and-a-half times farther on the surface?

☐ A. 20
☐ B. 35
☐ C. 60
☐ D. 175
☐ E. 315

10. When Peter and Bill ran a 100-metre race, Peter won by five metres. They raced again, but this time Peter started five metres behind the starting line. Assuming each man ran both races at the same speed, what were the results of the second race?

☐ A. Peter wins
☐ B. Bill wins
☐ C. It was a tie
☐ D. It can't be determined

11. John and Michael both earned the same amount. Last year John had a rise of ten per cent and Michael had a drop in pay of ten per cent. This year John had a ten per cent drop in pay and Michael had a ten per cent rise. Who is making more now?

☐ A. John
☐ B. Michael
☐ C. They are both earning the same amount
☐ D. It can't be determined

12 Clock A says it's 8:00, clock B says it's 8:50, and clock C says it's 8:20. One of the clocks is 20 minutes fast, one

is slow, and one is off by half an hour. What is the actual time?

- ☐ A. 8:00
- ☐ B. 8:15
- ☐ C. 8:23
- ☐ D. 8:30
- ☐ E. 8:41
- ☐ F. It can't be determined

13. Two people can make two bicycles in two hours. How many people are needed to make 12 bicycles in six hours?

- ☐ A. 2
- ☐ B. 3
- ☐ C. 4
- ☐ D. 5
- ☐ E. 6

14. A store reduced the price of one of its products by 25 per cent. What percentage of the reduced price must it be increased by to put the product back to its original price?

- ☐ A. 25 per cent
- ☐ B. 30 per cent
- ☐ C. 33 per cent
- ☐ D. 50 per cent
- ☐ E. 66 per cent

15. A box contains two coins. One coin is heads on both sides and the other is heads on one side and tails on the other. One coin is selected from the box at random and the face of one side is observed. If the face is heads what is the per cent chance that the other side is heads?

- ☐ A. 25 per cent
- ☐ B. 33 per cent
- ☐ C. 50 per cent
- ☐ D. 66 per cent
- ☐ E. 88 per cent

16. There are a total of ten bicycles and tricycles. If the total number of wheels is 24, how many are tricycles?

- ☐ A. 2
- ☐ B. 3
- ☐ C. 4
- ☐ D. 5
- ☐ E. 6

17. What is the product of the least common multiple and the greatest common factor of 15 and 24?

- ☐ A. 30
- ☐ B. 90
- ☐ C. 180
- ☐ D. 360
- ☐ E. 540

18. 1.28 can also be expressed as:

- ☐ A. 1 1/3
- ☐ B. 32/25
- ☐ C. 128/256
- ☐ D. 16/12
- ☐ E. 49/37

19. Which of the following is less than 1/6?

- ☐ A. 0.1667
- ☐ B. 3/18
- ☐ C. 0.167
- ☐ D. 0.1666
- ☐ E. 8/47

20. Which of the following fractions is closest in value to the decimal 0.31?

- ☐ A. 5/16
- ☐ B. 11/32
- ☐ C. 1/4

☐ D. 3/8
☐ E. 7/16

21. Which of the following numbers is evenly divisible by 6?

☐ A. 106
☐ B. 124
☐ C. 138
☐ D. 146
☐ E. 152

22. Which of the following is not a prime number?

☐ A. 53
☐ B. 59
☐ C. 61
☐ D. 67
☐ E. 72

23. What is the greatest integer that will divide evenly into both 36 and 54?

☐ A. 6
☐ B. 9
☐ C. 12
☐ D. 18
☐ E. 27

24. If the average of x and 9 is 7, then x equals:

☐ A. 3
☐ B. 5
☐ C. 6
☐ D. 7
☐ E. 9

25. In a certain pet store there are 24 gerbils and 9 hamsters. What is the ratio of hamsters to gerbils?

- [ ] A. 1: 4
- [ ] B. 1:3
- [ ] C. 3:8
- [ ] D. 2:3
- [ ] E. 3:4

26. If the ratio of boys to girls at a dance is 5:3, and there are 65 boys, how many girls must there be at the dance?

- [ ] A. 13
- [ ] B. 18
- [ ] C. 26
- [ ] D. 36
- [ ] E. 39

27. On a street map, 3/4 of a centimetre represents one kilometre. What distance, in kilometres, is represented by 1¾ centimetres?

- [ ] A. 1½
- [ ] B. 2
- [ ] C. 2⅓
- [ ] D. 2½
- [ ] E. 2⅝

28. A ship floats with 3/5 of its weight above the water. What is the ratio of the ship's submerged weight to its exposed weight?

- [ ] A. 3:8
- [ ] B. 2:5
- [ ] C. 3:5
- [ ] D. 2:3
- [ ] E. 5:3

29. Two hundred per cent more than 50 is:

- [ ] A. 100
- [ ] B. 150

☐. C. 175
☐ D. 200
☐ E. 250

30. 30 per cent of 10 is 10 per cent of what number?

☐ A. 10
☐ B. 15
☐ C. 30
☐ D. 60
☐ E. 300

31. The price of gum rises from 5p to 15p. What is the per cent increase in price?

☐ A. 50 per cent
☐ B. 75 per cent
☐ C. 100 per cent
☐ D. 150 per cent
☐ E. 200 per cent

32. John bought a painting for £8,000. If he sells it for a profit of 12.5 per cent of the original cost, what is the selling price of the painting?

☐ A. £8,125
☐ B. £8,800
☐ C. £9,000
☐ D. £9,500
☐ E. £10,000

33. If $3^x = 81$ then $x^3 = ?$

☐ A. 12
☐ B. 16
☐ C. 64
☐ D. 81
☐ E. 128

34. Which of the following is not a prime number?

- ☐ A. 5
- ☐ B. 7
- ☐ C. 9
- ☐ D. 11
- ☐ E. 13

35. Which type of triangle has all three sides of different lengths and all three angles of different sizes?

- ☐ A. Scalene
- ☐ B. Isosceles
- ☐ C. Equilateral
- ☐ D. Acute
- ☐ E. Obtuse

36. Which holds more, an American quart, a British quart, or a litre?

- ☐ A. American quart
- ☐ B. British quart
- ☐ C. Litre
- ☐ D. They all hold the same

37. What does the letter L represent in Roman numerals?

- ☐ A. 5
- ☐ B. 50
- ☐ C. 100
- ☐ D. 500
- ☐ E. 1000

38. A hexagon has how many sides?

- ☐ A. 4
- ☐ B. 6
- ☐ C. 8
- ☐ D. 0
- ☐ E. 12

Answer key

1.	D	14.	C	27.	C
2.	C	15.	D	28.	D
3.	C	16.	C	29.	B
4.	C	17.	D	30.	C
5.	B	18.	B	31.	E
6.	A	19.	D	32.	C
7.	B	20.	A	33.	C
8.	D	21.	C	34.	C
9.	A	22.	E	35.	A
10.	A	23.	D	36.	B
11.	C	24.	B	37.	B
12.	D	25.	C	38.	B
13.	C	26.	E		

How to score this test

Raw Score	Mathematical IQ score
1	90
2	92
3	94
4	96
5	98
6	100
7	102
8	104
9	106
10	108
11	110
12	112
13	114
14	116
15	118
16	120
17	122
18	124
19	126

Raw Score	Mathematical IQ score
20	128
21	130
22	132
23	134
24	136
25	137
26	138
27	139
28	140
29	141
30	142
31	143
32	144
33	145
34	146
35	147
36	148
37	149
38	150+

Interpreting your score

Below you will find a bell curve graph with a range of IQ scores on the bottom and a brief description of each level. The percentages in the curve represent the rarity of such a score in the general population. For example, a score of 115 will put you in the top 16 per cent of the population.

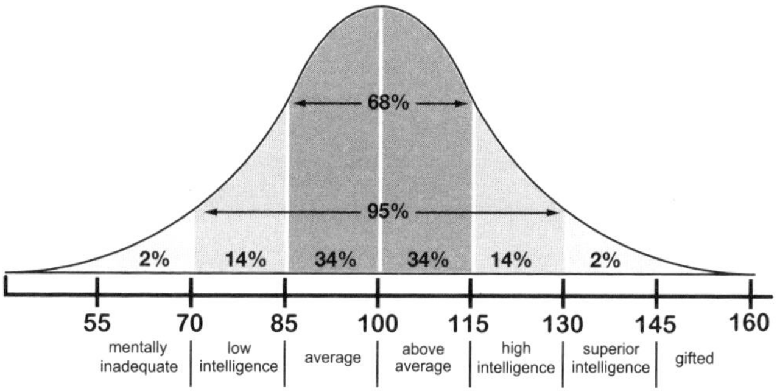

It's important to keep in mind that since this test is not given under controlled conditions, it cannot give a true IQ score. The score given on this test is intended merely as an indicator of how a person might perform on an IQ test.

Further reading

Handbook of Intelligence by Robert J. Sternberg

9

ASSESSING YOUR LOGICAL INTELLIGENCE

Assessing your logical intelligence

Logical intelligence is our ability to mentally process logical problems and equations, the type most often found on multiple choice standardized tests. Of all the different types of intelligences, this one is the most thoroughly documented and studied.

This intelligence uses numbers, maths and logic to arrive at the correct answer. If you happen to be a logical-mathematically inclined person you tend to think more conceptually and abstractly and are often able to see patterns and relationships that others miss. People with a high level of this intelligence tend to enjoy solving puzzles, working with numbers and mathematical formulas, and the challenge of a complex problem to solve.

A few ways to improve your logical-mathematical intelligence are to play games such as chess and Go, work on logic puzzles and brainteasers, and read books on recreational mathematics.

How to take the test

This test is designed to test your logic and mathematical IQ. It will assess your ability to solve mathematical and logic word problems. The test does not require mathematical education above secondary school level.

You are permitted to use a calculator and a piece of paper and a pen. There are 15 questions and you have 60 minutes to complete the test.

1. Chris loves the girl who is in love with Don. Jim loves the girl who loves the man who loves Gillian. Tom loves the girl who loves the man who loves Justine. Kim does not love Tom. Alice loves a man who does not love Kim. Who loves Justine?

☐ A. Chris
☐ B. Don
☐ C. Jim
☐ D. Tom
☐ E. None of the above

2. When Al and George ran a 100-metre race, Al won by five metres. So to give George a chance they raced again, but this time Al started five metres behind the starting line. Each man ran the race at the same speed as in the first race. What were the results of the second race?

☐ A. Al won
☐ B. George won
☐ C. It was a tie

3 A contractor estimated that one of his two bricklayers would take 9 hours to build a certain wall and the other 10 hours. When the two bricklayers worked together, however, 10 fewer bricks got laid per hour. With both men working on the job it took exactly 5 hours to build the wall. How many bricks did it contain?

☐ A. 680
☐ B. 860
☐ C. 900
☐ D. 1024
☐ E. None of the above

4. You have a can with four balls of different colours. Randomly, you draw two at a time, then paint the first ball to match the second. What is the expected number of drawings before all balls are the same colour?

- ☐ A. 6
- ☐ B. 7
- ☐ C. 8
- ☐ D. 9
- ☐ E. None of the above

5. Transport for London buys wheels for the London Underground for £200 per wheel. The wheels last for eight years and then they have a scrap value of £25 apiece. If rust-proofing treatment costing £60 a wheel is applied, each wheel will last twelve years but will have no scrap value. In the long run, would it be more cost-effective to rust-proof the wheels?

   - ☐ A. No
   - ☐ B. Yes
   - ☐ C. It is impossible to tell
   - ☐ D. It would cost the same

6. After graduating from college, Alison went to work for a financial firm and Eric went to work for a law firm, both earning the same amount. Last year Alison had a rise of ten per cent and Eric had a drop in pay of ten per cent. This year Alison had a ten per cent drop in pay and Eric had the ten per cent rise. Who is making more now?

   - ☐ A. Alison
   - ☐ B. Eric
   - ☐ C. They are both making the same
   - ☐ D. It is impossible to tell

7. Both Aaron and Alexander hit their target fifty per cent of the time. They decide to fight a duel in which they exchange alternate shots until one is hit. What are the odds of the man who shoots first?

   - ☐ A. 1/2
   - ☐ B. 3/8
   - ☐ C. 2/3

(continued)

- ☐ D. 5/8
- ☐ E. None of the above

8. Five suspects were rounded up in connection with a robbery. Their statements were as follows:

Alex: “Chris and Dave are lying.”
Brad: “Alex and Eric are lying.”
Chris: “Brad and Dave are lying.”
Dave: “Chris and Eric are lying.”
Eric: “Alex and Brad are lying.”
Who is the only suspect we know with certainty to be lying?

- ☐ A. Alex
- ☐ B. Brad
- ☐ C. Chris
- ☐ D. Dave
- ☐ E. Eric

9. If Erin is as old as Lisa will be when Bippy is as old as Erin is now, who is the oldest?

- ☐ A. Erin
- ☐ B. Lisa
- ☐ C. Bippy

10. In a certain community there are 1,000 married couples. Two-thirds of the husbands who are taller than their wives are also heavier, and three-quarters of the husbands who are heavier than their wives are also taller. If there are 120 wives who are taller and heavier than their husbands, how many husbands are taller and heavier than their wives?

- ☐ A. 340
- ☐ B. 480
- ☐ C. 240
- ☐ D. 120
- ☐ E. None of the above

11. A woman spent one-sixth of her life in childhood, one-twelfth in youth, and one-seventh as a single woman. Five years after she got married, a son was born who died four years before his mother at half his mother's final age. What was the woman's final age?

12. A cereal company is offering a harmonica to anyone who sends in enough box tops. Gillian and Tess each want a harmonica. Tess needs seven more box tops and Gillian needs one more. They thought of combining their box tops to get one harmonica, but they still don't have enough. How many box tops are needed for one harmonica?

13. Wyman went shopping. At a shoe shop he spent half of what he had plus £6 for a pair of trainers. At a clothing store he spent half of what was left plus £4 for a sweater. At the bookshop he spent half of what remained plus £2 for a calculator. He had £7 left over. How much did he have originally?

- ☐ A. £50
- ☐ B. £80
- ☐ C. £110
- ☐ D. £135
- ☐ E. None of the above

14. There are nine jars, each containing a different type of liquid, but the labels have all fallen off. Knowing nothing about the contents, a passer-by reapplies the labels at random. What is the expected number of correctly labelled jars?

- ☐ A. 1
- ☐ B. 2
- ☐ C. 3
- ☐ D. 4
- ☐ E. 5

15. At a hardware store you can buy bolts in boxes of 6, 9, and 20. What is the largest number such that you cannot order any combination of the above to achieve exactly the number you want?

How to score this test

This test was developed with a specific weighting for each question. Some are harder than others and this is reflected in the weighting. The weighting for each question can be from 100 to 1,000, with 1,000 being the most difficult.

Use the answer key to find out which questions you answered correctly and write down the weighting points associated with the correct answer. Only award yourself points for the questions which you answered correctly.

Once you have added up all your points, see the scoring diagram which follows the answer key to determine your overall logical intelligence score based on your total points.

Question number	Correct number	Question weighting
1	A	770 points
2	A	460 points
3	C	470 points
4	D	770 points
5	B	320 points
6	C	300 points
7	C	690 points
8	A	500 points
9	A	270 points
10	B	580 points
11	84	630 points
12	7	450 points
13	E	320 points
14	A	590 points
15	43	930 points
TOTAL		

Scoring diagram

90	100
91	200
92	300
93	400
94	500
95	600
96	700
97	800
98	900
99	1000
100	1100
101	1200
102	1300
103	1400
104	1500
105	1600
106	1700
107	1800
108	1900
109	2000
110	2100
111	2200
112	2300
113	2400
114	2500
115	2600
116	2700

117	2800
118	2900
119	3000
120	310
121	3200
122	3300
123	3400
124	3500
125	3600
126	3700
127	3800
128	3900
129	4000
130	4100
131	4200
132	4300
133	4400
134	4500
135	4600
136	4700
137	4800
138	4900
139	5000
140	5100
141	5200
142	5300
143	5400

144	5500
145	5600
146	5700
147	5800
148	5900
149	6000
150	6100
151	6200
152	6300
153	6400
154	6500
155	6600
156	6700
157	6800
158	6900
159	7000
160	7100
161	7200
162	7300
163	7400
164	7500
165	7600
166	7700
167	7800
168	7900
169	8000
170+	8100

Further reading

On Intelligence by Jeff Hawkins and Sandra Blakeslee

10

ASSESSING YOUR VISUAL-SPATIAL INTELLIGENCE

Assessing your visual-spatial intelligence

Visual-spatial intelligence relies on pictures and images rather than on words. Visual-spatial people think visually and are better at remembering things they have read than things that they are told. Visual-spatial thinking is more common in right-brain and perceptive personality types.

The concept of spatial ability comprised several components such as mental rotation, spatial perception, and spatial visualization. In most of these components there is a significant gap between female and male scores. The least sexually biased of the components is spatial visualization – or visual-spatial – which involves multi-step manipulations of spatially presented information. It is for this reason that we have decided to create a test that focuses exclusively on visuo-spatial patterns.

While other types of intelligence, such as mathematical and verbal, tend to receive the most attention and are often the most coveted, spatial ability is probably one of the most vital aspects of a person's capabilities. After all, without the ability to comprehend and interpret visual information, something as simple as remembering how to get from your bedroom to the kitchen would be too difficult a task to manage.

Spatial ability has long been recognized as a contributing factor to success in mathematics, natural sciences, engineering, and architecture. Having the ability to visualize the structure of complex molecules in chemistry, understand the interactions of mechanical systems in engineering, and interpret X-ray pictures in radiology requires spatial ability. This could be a reason that spatial ability is becoming increasingly important as we move into a more technology-driven world.

Some characteristics of an individual with highly developed spatial ability are:

- Learns concepts all at once.

- Reads maps well.

- Must visualize words to spell them.
- Much better at keyboarding than handwriting.
- Has good long-term visual memory.
- Is better at maths reasoning than computation.
- Is a whole-part learner.

How to take the test

You are given a series of boxes with a set of patterns in them. You'll need to recognize what the pattern is and how it would continue to the last box, the one with the question mark in it. While it sounds simple, the pattern can often be very difficult to find and there are several "red herring" patterns designed to throw you off.

There are 24 questions and there is a time limit of 45 minutes.

BEGIN TEST

1.

A B C D

2.

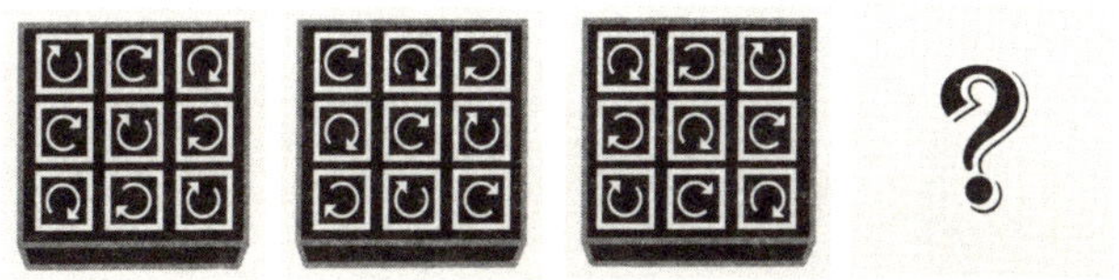

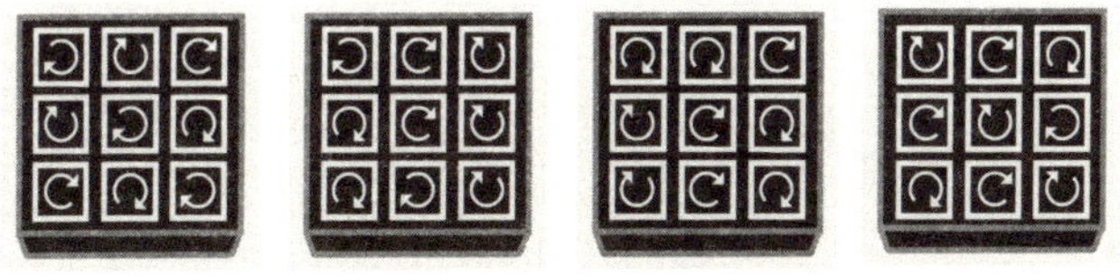

A B C D

3.

A B C D

4.

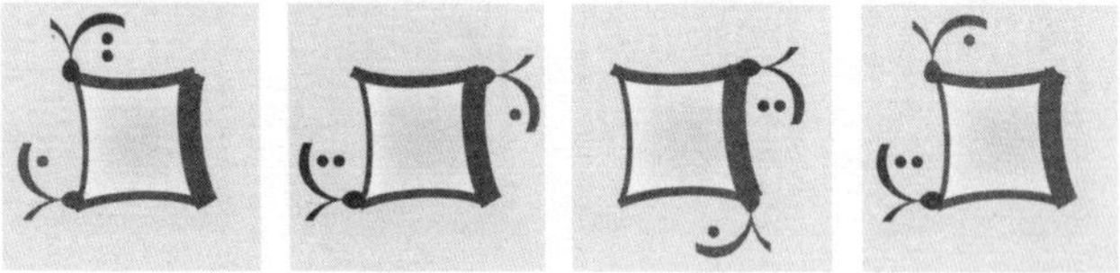

A B C D

5.

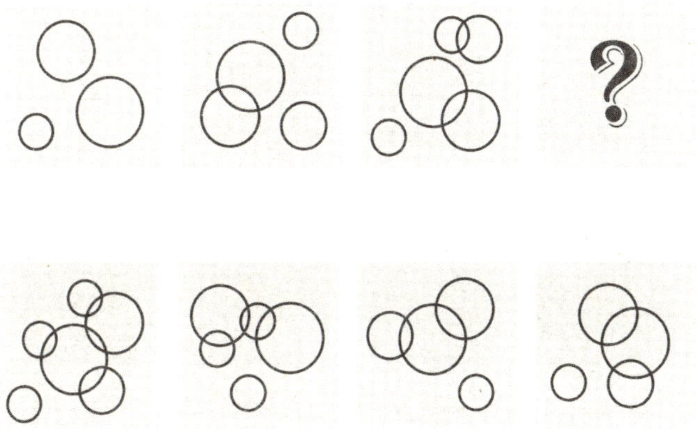

A B C D

6.

A B C D

7.

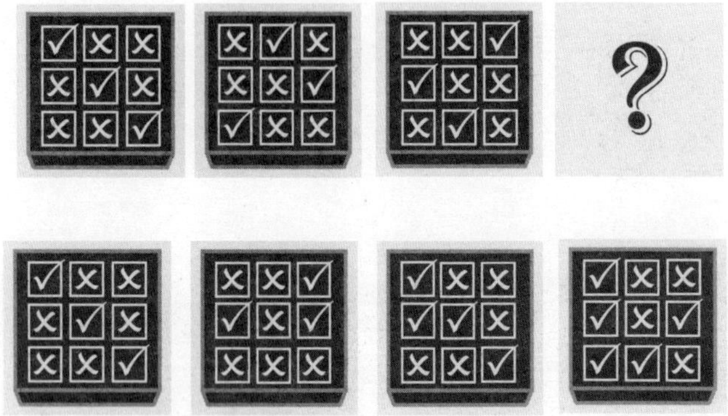

A B C D

8.

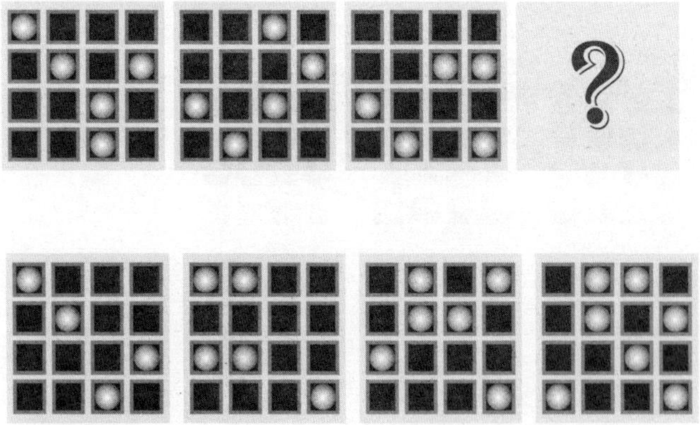

A B C D

9.

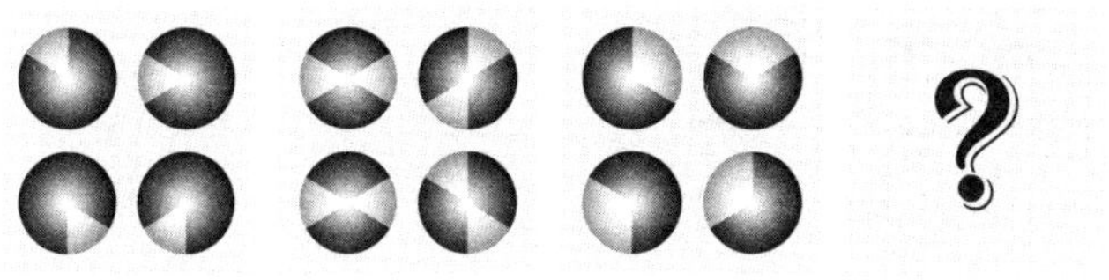

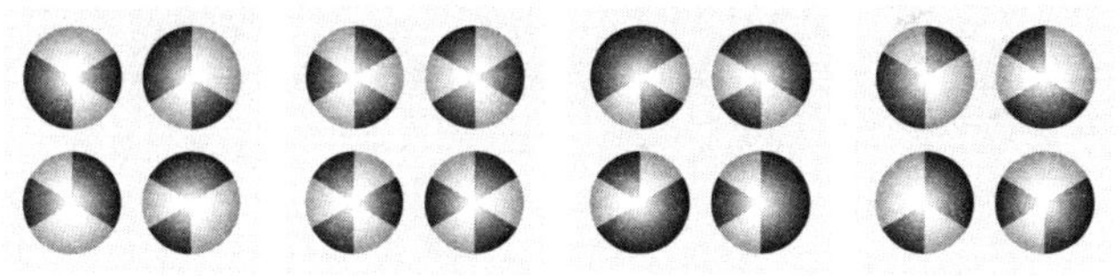

A B C D

10.

A B C D

11.

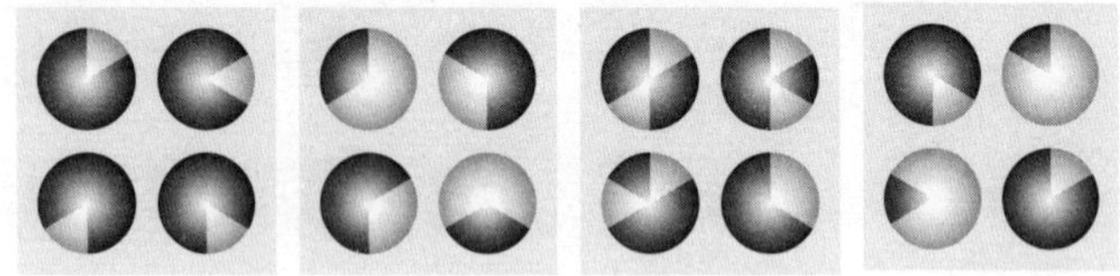

A B C D

12.

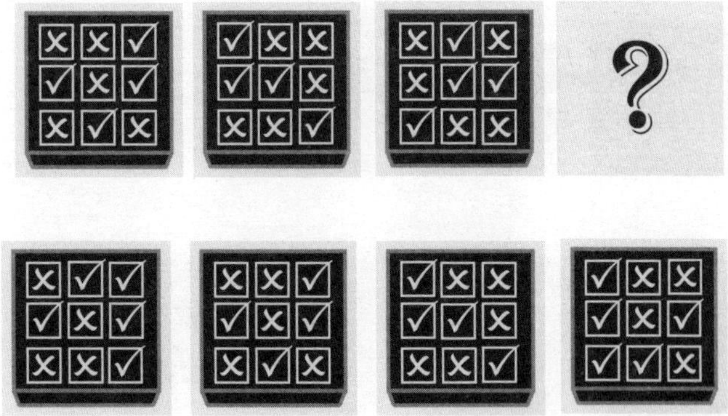

A B C D

13.

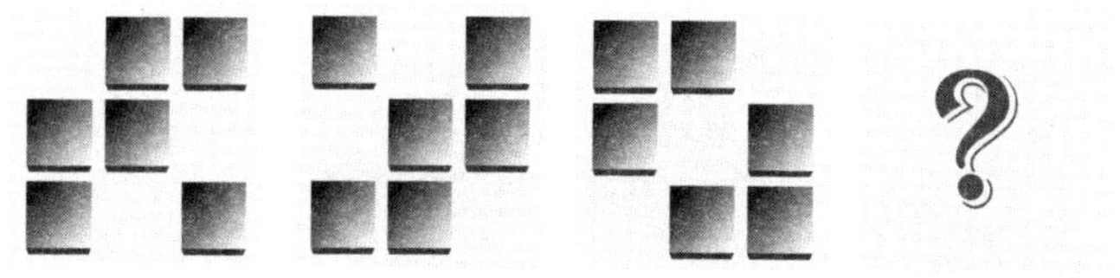

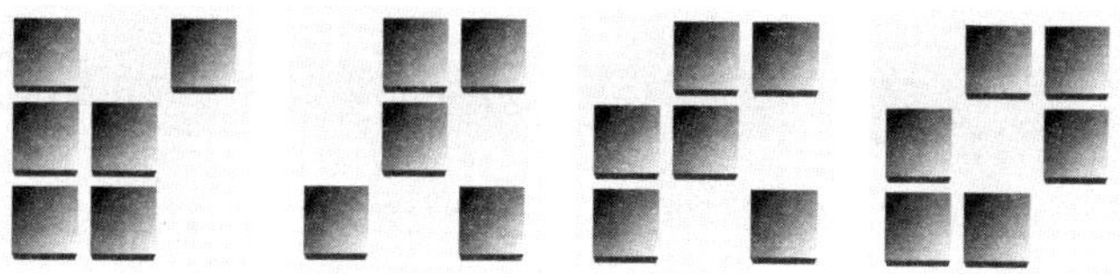

A B C D

14.

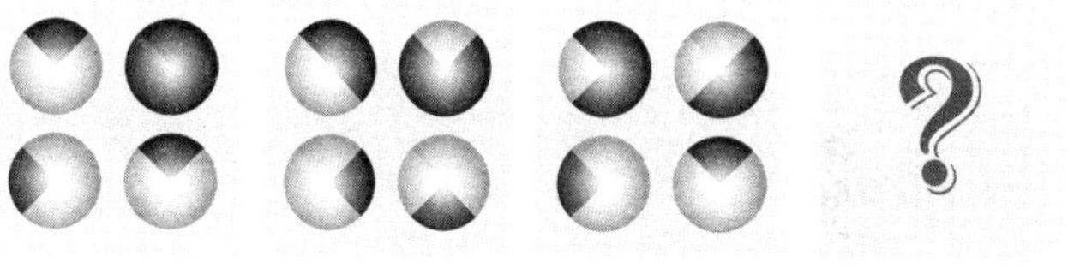

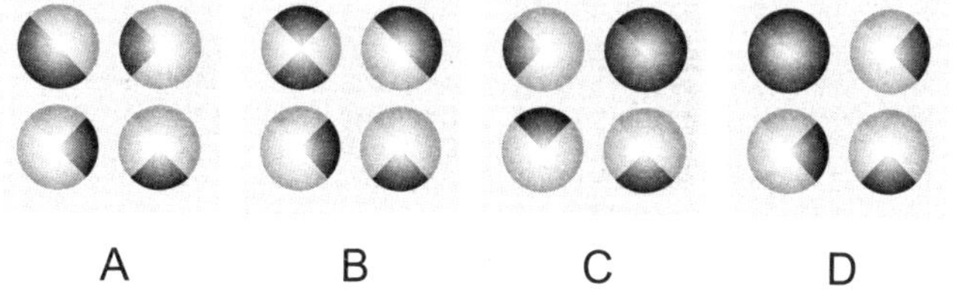

A B C D

15.

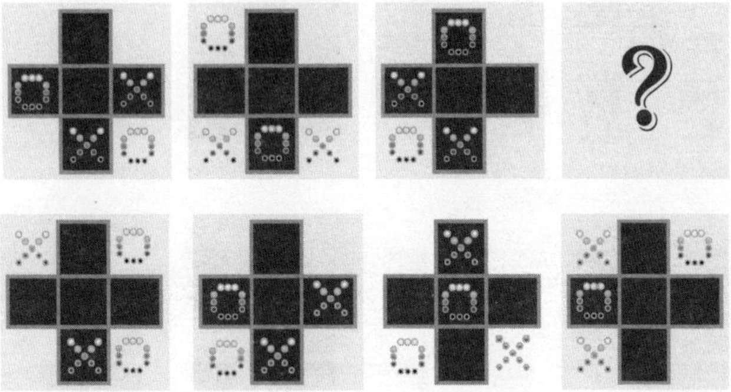

A B C D

16.

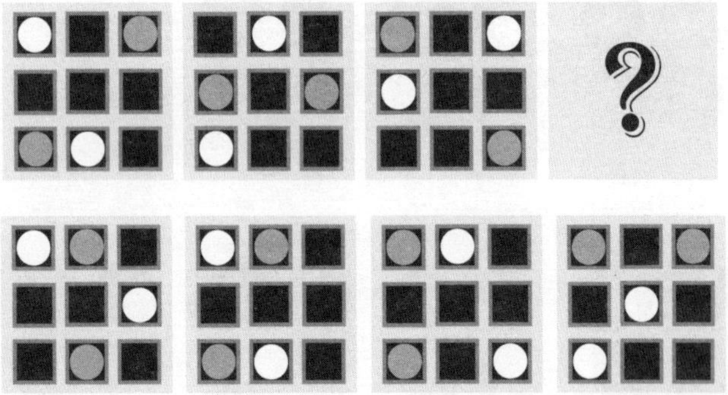

A B C D

17.

A B C D

18.

A B C D

19.

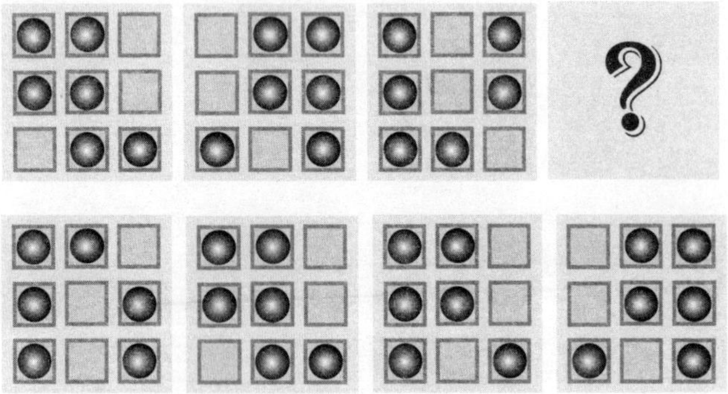

A B C D

20.

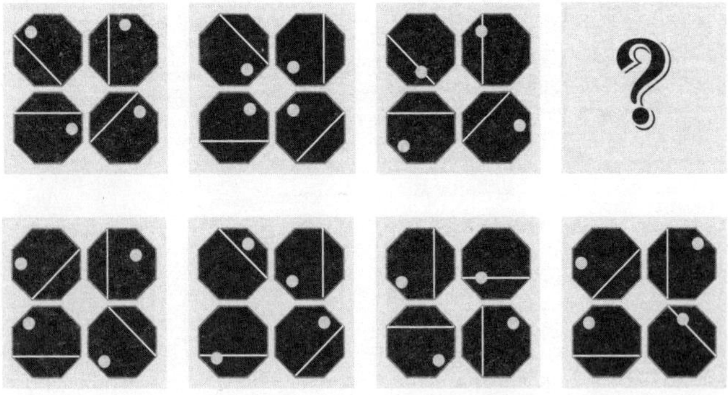

A B C D

21.

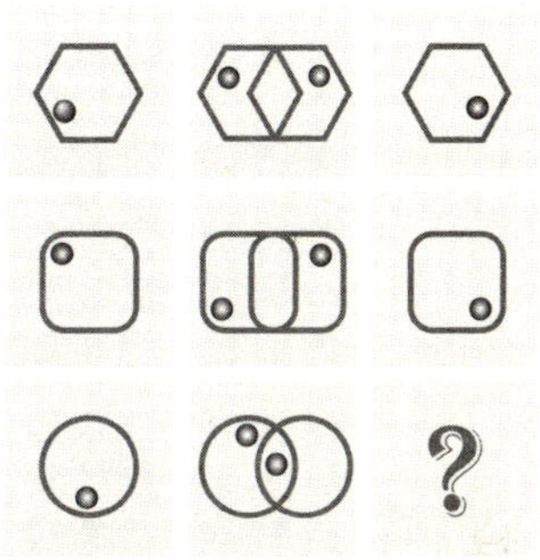

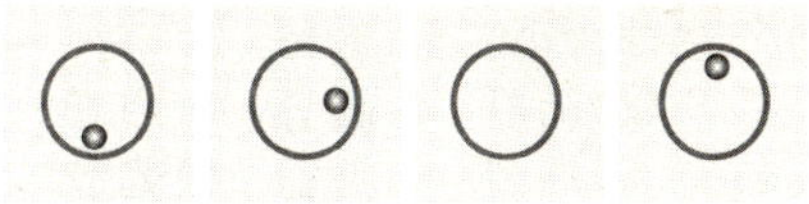

A B C D

22.

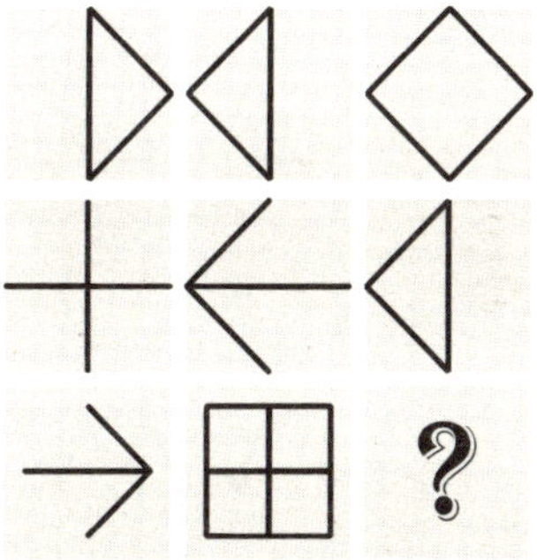

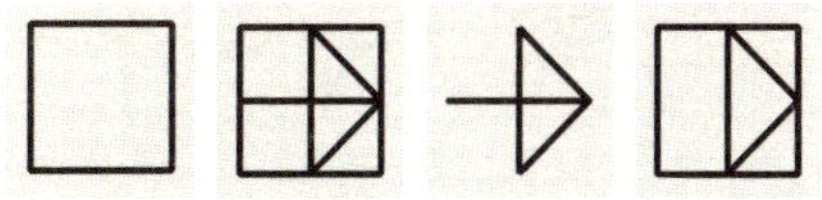

A B C D

23.

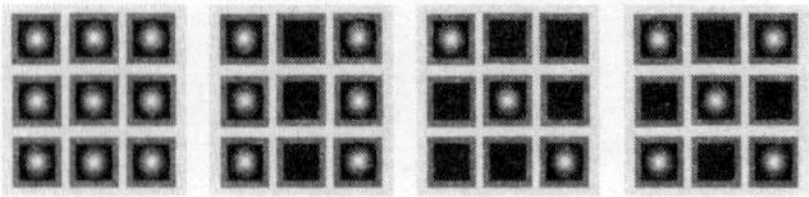

A B C D

24.

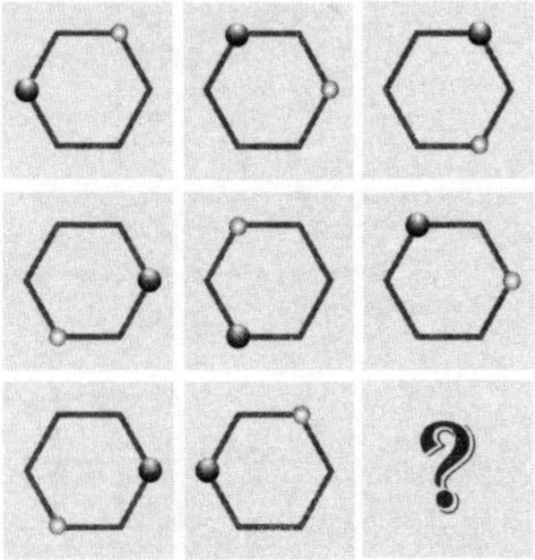

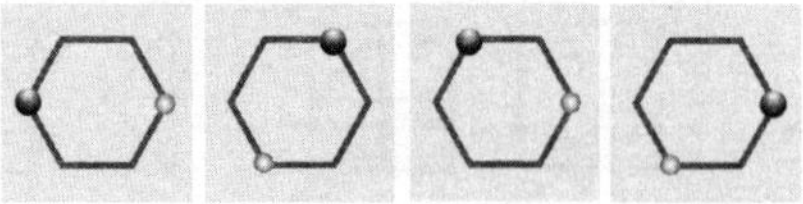

A B C D

Answer key

1.	D	9.	D	17.	C
2.	A	10.	D	18.	C
3.	A	11.	B	19.	B
4.	C	12.	B	20.	B
5.	B	13.	C	21.	B
6.	B	14.	D	22.	D
7.	A	15.	D	23.	A
8.	B	16.	A	24.	D

Answer key

Raw score	Visuospatial IQ score
1	90
2	94
3	98
4	100
5	102
6	106
7	108
8	112
9	114
10	118
11	120
12	124
13	128
14	130
15	134
16	137
17	138
18	140
19	142
20	144
21	146
22	148
23	149
24	150+

Interpreting your score

Below you will find a bell curve graph with a range of IQ scores on the bottom and a brief description of each level. The percentages in the curve represent the rarity of such a score in the general population. For example, a score of 115 will put you in the top 16 per cent of the population.

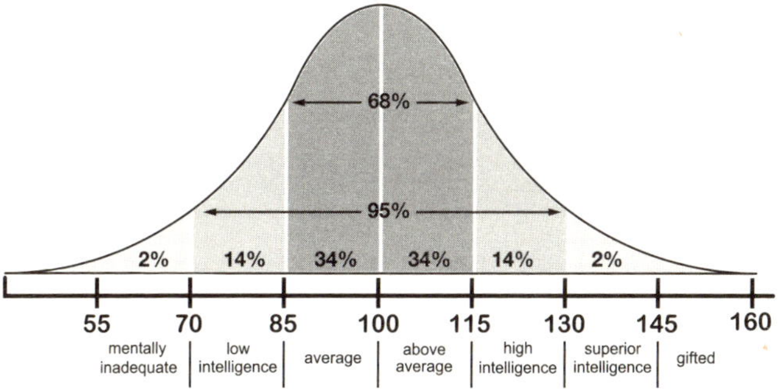

It's important to keep in mind that since this test is not given under controlled conditions, it cannot give a true IQ score. The score given on this test is intended merely as an indicator of how a person might perform on an IQ test.

Further reading

Visual Intelligence: How we create what we see by Donald D. Hoffman

11

ASSESSING YOUR VERBAL INTELLIGENCE

Assessing your verbal intelligence

Verbal intelligence is essentially the ability to use words and language. Those possessing a strong verbal intelligence tend to have highly developed skills for reading, speaking, and writing. An individual with a high verbal intelligence will have one or more of the following skills:

- The ability to use language as a tool for persuasion and to choose words well when writing and speaking.
- Understanding the meaning of words in both speech and writing and how to use the language properly.
- Understanding the various nuances of a language, including idioms, plays on words, and linguistically-based humour.

How to develop your verbal intelligence

There are many advantages to developing one's verbal intelligence. The following list of activities will help improve verbal intelligence. Read each item and try a few activities that you feel may help improve an area that you consider to be weak and that you would like to strengthen.

- Play word games.
- Join a book club.
- Visit the library and bookshops regularly.
- Join a speaker's club.
- Subscribe to a newspaper.
- Listen and watch recordings of famous orators.

- Keep a daily diary or journal.
- When reading, circle unfamiliar words and look them up.
- Buy a thesaurus and a style manual and use them regularly in your writing.
- Try to use at least one new word in your conversation every day.

How to take the test

What's your verbal IQ? Are you word-savvy? Do you have a natural ability with language? Find out where you stand with the Verbal Intelligence Test.

This test is designed for those whose first language is English. Take your time, read the questions carefully and choose the best response.

This test consists of 40 questions and you have 45 minutes in which to complete it.

Pencil and paper are allowed, but use of any reference material such as a dictionary, encyclopedia, or thesaurus is not allowed.

1. Can the word FLOURISHES be spelt using only the letters found in the word SUPERFLUOUS?

2. COOK is to KITCHEN as DRIVER is to:

   ☐ A. Office
   ☐ B. Building
   ☐ C. Hospital
   ☐ D. Truck
   ☐ E. Garden

3. If the word FISH is written under the word TIME and the word LINK is written under the word FISH and the word OBEY is written under the word LINK is the word TINY formed diagonally?

4. EJECT and REJECT are:

   ☐ A. Similar
   ☐ B. Dissimilar
   ☐ C. Opposite

5. Which of the following words is closest in meaning to abrogate?

   ☐ A. Abet
   ☐ B. Annul
   ☐ C. Redo
   ☐ D. Advocate

6. "Bip bop bup" means "we are healthy".
   "Bap bep bup" means "we like clouds".
   "Byp bap bop" means "clouds are coming".

   What words would you use to say: "We are coming"? The order that you place the words in is unimportant – you only need to find the correct words to use.

7. Do the consonants in the word BECKONERS appear in alphabetical order?

8. Change the first letter of each word to form a new word, using the same letter for both words on each line, and place the new letter between the parentheses to form a new word vertically.

GRID	( )	NIL
HEN	( )	LEAN
CART	( )	RAIN
CONS	( )	ONTO
BAIL	( )	DENT

9. BIRD is to AIR as FISH is to:

- ☐ A. Boat
- ☐ B. Shark
- ☐ C. Ship
- ☐ D. Sea
- ☐ E. Whale

10. Can the word BLEMISHED be spelt using only the letters found in the word ESTABLISHMENT?

11. Is the following sentence spelt the same forwards as it is backwards?

Bust to hot stub.

12. Do the vowels in the word UNFORGIVABLE appear in reverse alphabetical order?

13. Does the following sentence make sense if the word "suce" is understood to mean the same as the word "cook"? Although the suce had never suced before for an important event, he suced a really good meal.

14. Do the words, "singers, signers, and resigns" all use the exact same letters?

15. Is the nineteenth vowel appearing in this sentence the letter e?

16. Can the word TRACTOR be spelt by using the first letters of the words in the following sentence: Terrible reaction aroused by contracting of tracks over the river?

17. In the English alphabet, how many letters are there between the letter G and the letter K?

18. Does the following sentence make sense if the word "morder" is understood to mean the same as the word "go"? I don't think it's a good idea to morder there, because last time we mordered at that place we had a bad experience.

19. Do the words, "rises, sires, series" all use the exact same letters?

20. Is the eleventh vowel appearing in this sentence the letter e?

21. Can the word WATCHES be spelt by using the first letters of the words in the following sentence: Werewolves are the craziest habitual sleepers?

22. In the English alphabet, how many letters are there between the letter E and the letter H?

23. If the word DEAD is written under the word MADE and the word FEAR is written under the word DEAD and the word WELL is written under the word FEAR is the word MEAL formed diagonally?

24. Is the eleventh vowel appearing in this sentence the letter i?

25. If you remove ten letters from the word UNFORTUNATELY, can the word TALE be formed?

26. In the English alphabet, how many letters are there between the letter G and the letter X?

27. Change the first letter of each word to form a new word, using the same letter for both words on the same line, and place the new letter between the parentheses to form a new word vertically.

NOSE	( )	HOT
INCLOSE	( )	UNLISTED
PIECE	( )	TIGHT
KILT	( )	CUBE

28. Which of the following words is closest in meaning to exile?

- ☐ A. Trip
- ☐ B. Travel
- ☐ C. Ban
- ☐ D. Holiday

29. If the word DOCK is written under the word FAKE and the word TOLL is written under the word DOCK and the word FORK is written under the word TOLL is the word FOLK formed diagonally?

30. "Mip mop mup" means "you are ready".
"Map mip mep" means "better be ready".
"Myp map mop" means "tourists are better".

What words would you use to say: "Better be tourists"? The order that you place the words in is unimportant – you only need to find the correct words to use.

31. If all Gannucks are Dorks and most Gannucks are Xorgs, the statement that some Dorks are Xorgs is:

- ☐ A. True
- ☐ B. False
- ☐ C. Indeterminable from data

32. RECEIVE and CONCEIVE are:

- ☐ A. Similar
- ☐ B. Dissimilar
- ☐ C. Opposite

33. MOTHERBOARD is to COMPUTER as ATOMIC NUCLEUS is to:

- ☐ A. Proton
- ☐ B. Neutron
- ☐ C. Molecule
- ☐ D. Atom
- ☐ E. Vulcan

34. If most Trippers are Neatnicks and most Neatnicks are Notwants, the statement that some Neatnicks are Notwants is:

- ☐ A. True
- ☐ B. False
- ☐ C. Indeterminable from data

35. Is the tenth vowel appearing in this sentence the letter i?

36. Does the following sentence make sense if the word "larp" is understood to mean the same as the word "drive." All experienced larpers think that larping is easy when they larp on a good road.

37. If you remove seven letters from the word COMBINATION, can the word TOMB be formed?

38. If the word MALE is written under the word SEEM and the word BRIM is written under the word MALE and the

word WELL is written under the word BRIM is the word SALE formed diagonally?

39. Which of the following words is closest in meaning to opulent?

- ☐ A. Nice
- ☐ B. Happy
- ☐ C. Lavish
- ☐ D. Horrid

40. If you remove eight letters from the word ACKNOWLEDGEMENT, can the word ELEMENT be formed?

How to score this test

Use the answer key overleaf to work out how many questions you answered correctly. Once you've determined the total number of questions answered correctly proceed to the next page to determine your score.

Answer key

1. No
2. D
3. Yes
4. B
5. B
6. Bup bop byp
7. Yes
8. A D M I T

ARID	(A)	AIL
DEN	(D)	DEAN
MART	(M)	MAIN
IONS	(I)	INTO
TAIL	(T)	TENT

9. D
10. No
11. No
12. No
13. Yes
14. Yes
15. Yes
16. Yes
17. 3
18. No
19. No
20. No
21. No
22. 2
23. Yes
24. Yes
25. No
26. 16
27. R E N T

ROSE	(R)	ROT
ENCLOSE	(E)	ENLISTED
NIECE	(N)	NIGHT
TILT	(T)	TUBE

28. C
29. Yes
30. Map mep myp
31. A
32. B
33. D
34. A
35. Yes
36. Yes
37. Yes
38. No
39. C
40. Yes

Determining your level of verbal intelligence

In column A locate the number of correct answers you received on the test. Column B will show you your verbal intelligence IQ.

A	B
0	<70
1	70
2	72
3	74
4	76
5	78
6	80
7	82
8	84
9	86
10	88
11	90
12	92
13	94
14	96
15	98
16	100
17	102
18	104
19	106
20	108
21	110
22	112
23	114
24	116
25	118
26	120
27	122
28	124
29	126
30	128
31	130
32	132
33	134
34	136
35	138
36	140
37	142
38	144
39	146
40	150+

Interpreting your score

Below you will find a bell curve graph with a range of IQ scores on the bottom and a brief description of each level. The percentages in the curve represent the rarity of such a score in the general population. For example, a score of 115 will put you in the top 16 per cent of the population.

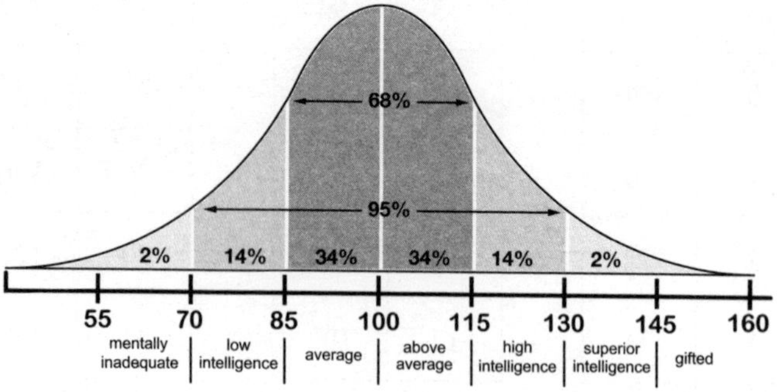

It's important to keep in mind that since this test is not given under controlled conditions, it cannot give a true IQ score. The score given on this test is intended merely as an indicator of how a person might perform on an IQ test.

Further reading

The Power of Verbal Intelligence by Tony Buzan

12

ASSESSING YOUR LATERAL THINKING

Assessing your lateral thinking

Lateral thinking is simply the generation of novel solutions to problems. The point of lateral thinking is that many problems require a different perspective to solve successfully.

Unlike most puzzles, lateral thinking puzzles are inexact and combine storytelling with puzzles. An example of a lateral thinking puzzle would be: A man rode into town on Friday. He stayed for three nights and then left on Friday. How is this possible? Initially the brain starts thinking vertically and is trying to visualize a calendar or some other way to solve it. When you step outside the confines of a traditional puzzle and try to find a different perspective, you might come up with the answer, which is the man's horse was named Friday. To get a different perspective on these problems, try breaking the elements up and recombining them in a different way (perhaps randomly).

How to take the test

The following questions will test your ability to think laterally. In each puzzle basic clues to a scenario are given, but the clues don't tell the full story. Your objective is to fill in the details and have the resulting scenario make sense. There is usually more than one answer to any given puzzle, but, in general, only the solution given is truly satisfying.

There are 25 questions and there is no time limit.

BEGIN TEST

1. A man arrived early to a party and drank some of the punch. He decided to leave early as well. Everyone else at the party who drank the punch subsequently died of poisoning. Why did the man not die?

2. There were two men drinking in a bar when two women walked in. The first man said, "I have to go, my wife and daughter are here." The second man turned around and said, "I have to go too, my wife and daughter just arrived as well." How is this possible?

3. Two Americans are standing in line to get on a flight to Canada. One of them is the father of the other's son. How is this possible?

4. A man lives on the 20th floor of a block of flats. If it is a rainy day, he gets into the lift in the morning, goes down to the ground floor and goes off to work. In the afternoon when he comes home, he gets into the lift and goes straight to the 20th floor. However, if it is a sunny day he goes down to the ground floor in the morning, but when he comes home he only goes up to the 10th floor and then walks up 10 flights of stairs. Why does he do this?

5. A man is hanging from a rope in a locked room with no furniture. Below him is a puddle of water. How did he hang himself?

6. Two men went into a restaurant. They both ordered the same dish from the menu. After tasting it, one of the men knew that he had eaten his friend. How did he know?

7. A man wakes up one morning, looks out of his window, and knows that he has caused the deaths of hundreds of people. How does he know?

8. Five pieces of coal, a carrot and a scarf are lying on the lawn. Nobody put them on the lawn but there is a

perfectly logical reason why they should be there. What is it?

9. A man walked into a bar and asked the barman for a glass of water. The barman pulled out a gun and pointed it at the man. The man said, "Thank you," and walked out. Explain.

10. Every day a woman takes the bus to work. She can get off at one of two stops. The first stop is 100 metres from the office building in which she works. The second stop is 200 metres past the building. She always rides past the first stop, and gets off at the second. Why?

11. While hiking in the mountains, a man discovers a locked cabin with three people dead inside. How did they die?

12. A man died and went to heaven. There were millions of other people there, all completely naked. He looked around to see if there was anyone he recognized. He saw a couple and he knew immediately that they were Adam and Eve. How did he know?

13. A woman had two sons who were born on the same hour of the same day of the same year. But they were not twins. How can this be?

14. Those who make them don't need them. Those who buy them don't want them. And those who use them don't know it. What are they?

15. A man sitting on a park bench reads a newspaper article headlined "Death At Sea" and knows that a murder was committed. How does he know?

16. A hunter aimed his gun carefully, and pulled the trigger. Seconds later he realized his mistake. Minutes later he was dead. What happened?

17. A woman arrived home after shopping with her bag of groceries, walked into the house and picked up the post. On her way to the kitchen, she walked through the living room and looked at her husband, who had blown his brains out. She then continued into the kitchen, put away the groceries, and cooked her dinner. Explain.

18. There is a man dead in a locked office, sitting at his desk. On the desk there are a couple of pieces of blank paper, a pen, and a sealed envelope. How was he killed?

19. Three large people are crowding together under one small umbrella, yet nobody gets wet. How is this possible?

20. A heavyset man who works in the butcher's shop is 6' 2" tall. What does he weigh?

21. A horse jumps over a castle and lands on a man, who disappears. Explain.

22. Two men played five chess games each but both of them won three games. How is this possible?

23. A man goes into a hardware store and asks the owner for something. The owner responds, "Four will cost you £3, ten will cost you £6, and two hundred will cost £9." What is the man buying?

24. A man hails a taxi, gets in and gives the driver the destination address. The taxi sets out, but then the driver stops in a secluded place and the driver kills the man. Why?

25. A man marries twenty women in his town, but isn't charged with polygamy. Why?

Answer key

1 The poison in the punch came from the ice cubes. When the man drank the punch, the ice was fully frozen. Gradually it melted, poisoning the punch.

2. The two men in question were both widowers with a daughter from a previous marriage. They both married the other's daughter.

3. They are husband and wife.

4. The man is extremely short, so on any ordinary day he cannot reach further than the button for floor 10 in the lift. When it rains, he can use his umbrella to reach the lift button for floor 20.

5. The puddle is all that is left of a large block of ice. The man stood on this in order to hang himself.

6. The men had been shipwrecked on an island with some other people many years earlier. At that time, they had been given some soup and told that it was albatross soup. It was, in fact, cooked from the meat of a human friend who had "disappeared" earlier. The two soups had different tastes.

7. The man is a lighthouse keeper who forgot to turn the light on the previous evening. He sees the ships that have been shipwrecked during the night.

8. They are the eyes, nose, and scarf of a snowman. The snow has melted, leaving only these items in the middle of the field.

9. The man had hiccups. The barman recognized this from his speech and drew the gun in order to give him a shock. It cured the hiccups, so the man no longer needed the water.

10. Her office building is on a hill. When she gets off at the stop farthest from the building she is walking downhill.

11. The cabin is a plane's cockpit. The people are the flying crew, whose plane had crashed during the snowstorm the night before.

12. He recognized Adam and Eve as the only people without navels. Because they were not born, they had never had umbilical cords, and therefore they did not have navels.

13. They were two of a set of triplets.

14. Headstones.

15. The man is a travel agent. He had sold someone two tickets for an ocean voyage, one ticket round-trip and one ticket one-way. The surname of the woman who "fell" overboard and drowned on the voyage (as reported in the newspaper) is the same surname as that of the man who bought the tickets.

16. The hunter was near a snowy cliff. When he fired the gun, he "triggered" an avalanche which buried him.

17. Her husband had killed himself a few years ago, and it is the urn on the mantelpiece containing his ashes that the wife looks at.

18. The seal on the envelope was poisoned, so when he licked and sealed it, he was poisoned.

19. It isn't raining.

20. The heavyset man weighs meat.

21. It's a chess game. The move is "knight takes pawn."

22 The men didn't have five games against each other, just five games each.

23. The man was buying house numbers – each digit costs £3.

24. The taxi driver has suspicions that someone is having an affair with his wife while he works. The man asks to be taken to the driver's home address, where the wife is alone at home.

25. He's a priest and is marrying them to other people, not to himself.

Determining your level of ability as a lateral thinker

Number correct	Lateral thinking rank
0–3	Illogical
4–6	Laterally challenged
7–8	Critical thinker
9–11	Shrewd
12–14	Astute
15+	Sherlock Holmes!

Further reading

Lateral Thinking: Creativity step by step by Edward De Bono

13

TWELVE-MINUTE IQ TEST

The Twelve-minute IQ test is a timed test consisting of 30 questions assessing your verbal, mathematical, and visual-spatial skills. This test is a composite of three different tests, the verbal test, the mathematical test and the visual-spatial test. Components from each were selected and compiled into a speeded, time-sensitive test. This timed test is slightly speeded relative to the longer IQ tests in the book so it is sensitive to processing speed and you will need to pay close attention to the time limit if you want to ensure an accurate score. It's designed so that most people will run out of time before completing it. Don't worry about running out of time because the aim of the test isn't just to measure how well you do on the questions, but how well you do under a restrictive time limit.

It's important that you keep a close watch on the time and that you do not simply guess at the remaining answers a few seconds before time runs out. It's best to give each question your attention and answer to the best of your ability. When the time runs out, put down your pencil and tabulate your scores. No negative points are awarded to those questions you've left blank.

BEGIN TEST

1. If all Gannucks are Dorks and most Gannucks are Xorgs, the statement that some Dorks are Xorgs is:

☐ A. True
☐ B. False
☐ C. Indeterminable from data

2. RECEIVE and CONCEIVE are:

☐ A. Similar
☐ B. Dissimilar
☐ C. Opposite

3. MOTHERBOARD is to COMPUTER as ATOMIC NUCLEUS is to:

☐ A. Proton
☐ B. Neutron
☐ C. Molecule
☐ D. Atom
☐ E. Vulcan

4. If most Trippers are Neatnicks and most Neatnicks are Notwants, the statement that some Neatnicks are Notwants is:

☐ A. True
☐ B. False
☐ C. Indeterminable from data

5. Is the tenth vowel appearing in this sentence the letter i?

6. Does the following sentence makes sense if the word "larp" is understood to mean the same as the word "drive"? All experienced larpers think that larping is easy when they larp on a good road.

7. If you remove seven letters from the word COMBINATION, can the word TOMB be formed?

8. If the word MALE is written under the word SEEM and the word BRIM is written under the word MALE and the word WELL is written under the word BRIM, is the word SALE formed diagonally?

9. Which of the following words is closest in meaning to opulent?

- ☐ A. Nice
- ☐ B. Happy
- ☐ C. Lavish
- ☐ D. Horrid

10. If you remove eight letters from the word ACKNOWLEDGEMENT, can the word ELEMENT be formed?

11. Two hundred per cent more than 50 is:

- ☐ A. 100
- ☐ B. 150
- ☐ C. 175
- ☐ D. 200
- ☐ E. 250

12. 30 per cent of 10 is 10 per cent of what number?

- ☐ A. 10
- ☐ B. 15
- ☐ C. 30
- ☐ D. 60
- ☐ E. 300

13. The price of gum rises from 5p to 15p. What is the per cent increase in price?

- ☐ A. 50 per cent
- ☐ B. 75 per cent
- ☐ C. 100 per cent
- ☐ D. 150 per cent
- ☐ E. 200 per cent

14. John bought a painting for £8,000. If he sells it for a profit of 12.5 per cent of the original cost, what is the selling price of the painting?

- ☐ A. £8,125
- ☐ B. £8,800
- ☐ C. £9,000
- ☐ D. £9,500
- ☐ E. £10,000

15. If $3^x = 81$ then $x^3 = ?$

- ☐ A. 12
- ☐ B. 16
- ☐ C. 64
- ☐ D. 81
- ☐ E. 128

16. Which of the following is not a prime number?

- ☐ A. 5
- ☐ B. 7
- ☐ C. 9
- ☐ D. 11
- ☐ E. 13

17. Which type of triangle has all three sides of different lengths and all three angles of different sizes?

- ☐ A. Scalene
- ☐ B. Isosceles
- ☐ C. Equilateral
- ☐ D. Acute
- ☐ E. Obtuse

18. Which holds more, an American quart, a British quart, or a litre?

- ☐ A. American quart

- ☐ B. British quart
- ☐ C. Litre
- ☐ D. They all hold the same

19. What does the letter L represent in Roman numerals?

- ☐ A. 5
- ☐ B. 50
- ☐ C. 100
- ☐ D. 500
- ☐ E. 1000

20. A hexagon has how many sides?

- ☐ A. 4
- ☐ B. 6
- ☐ C. 8
- ☐ D. 10
- ☐ E. 12

21.

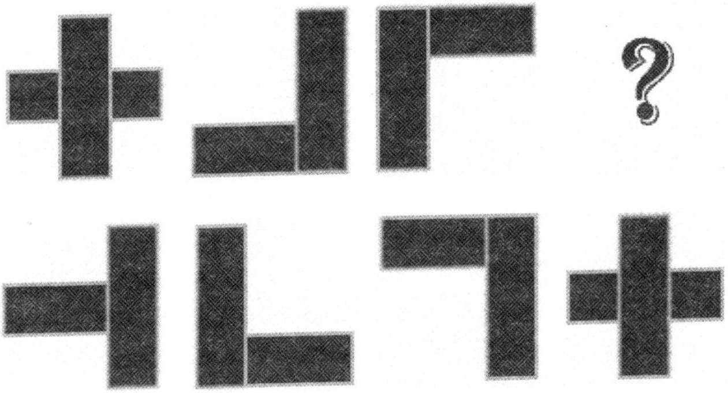

A B C D

22.

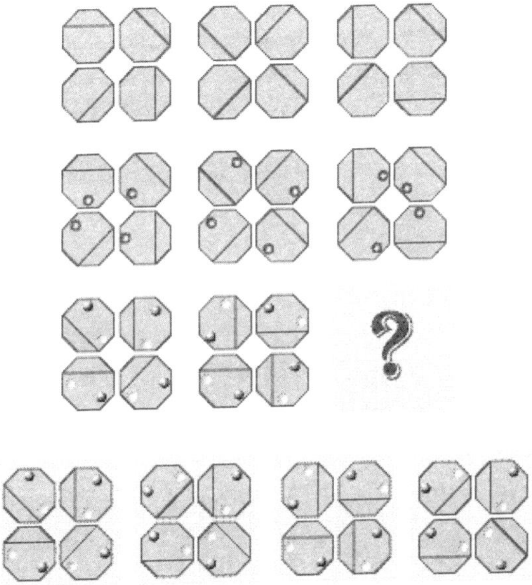

A B C D

23.

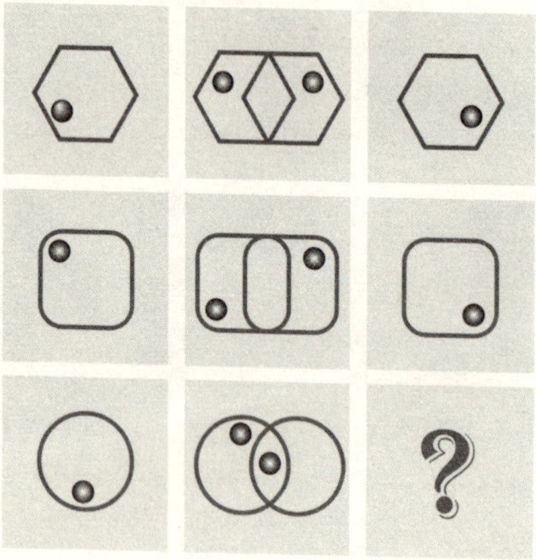

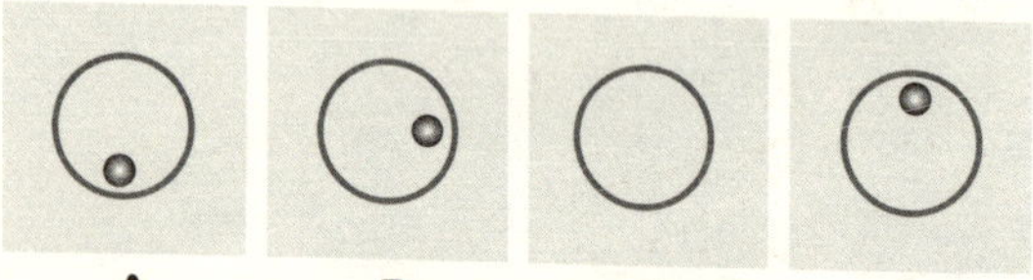

A B C D

24.

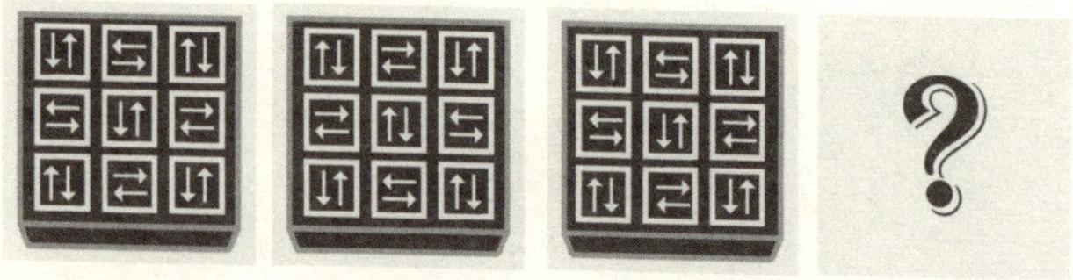

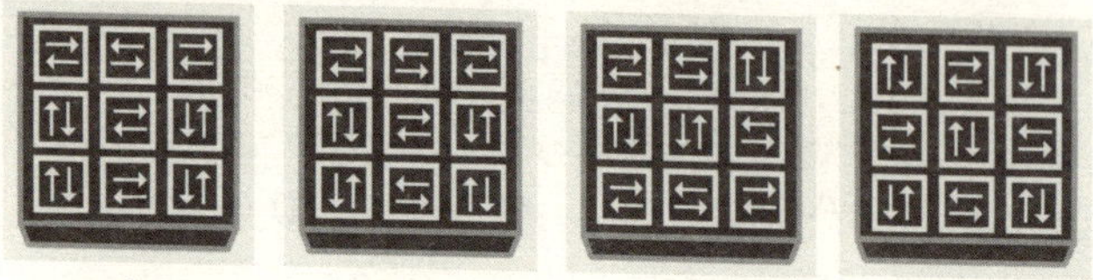

A B C D

25.

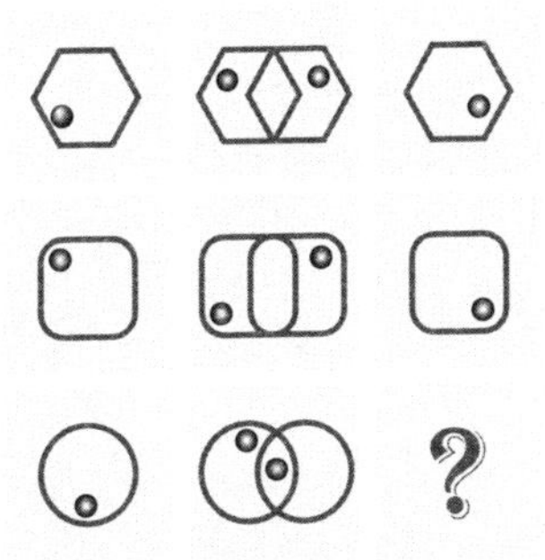

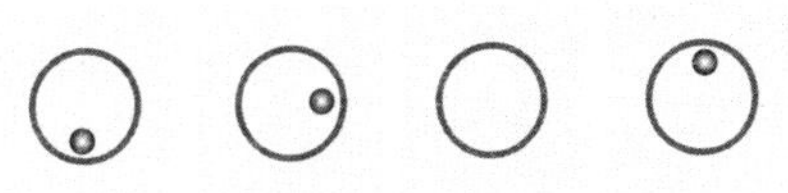

A B C D

26.

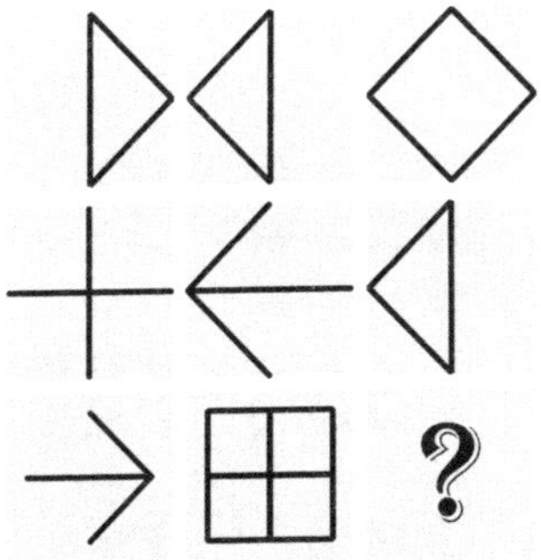

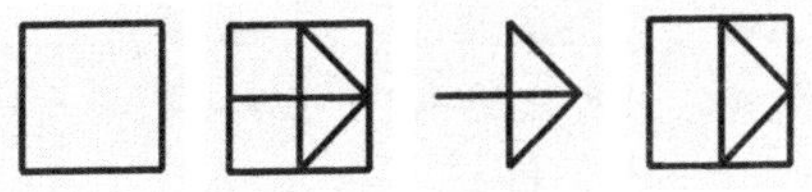

A B C D

27.

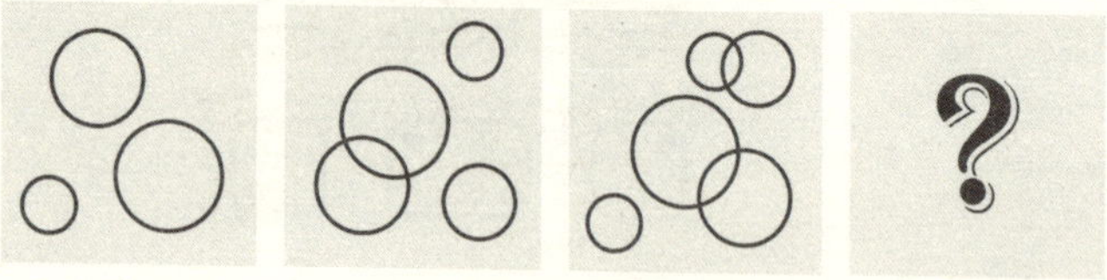

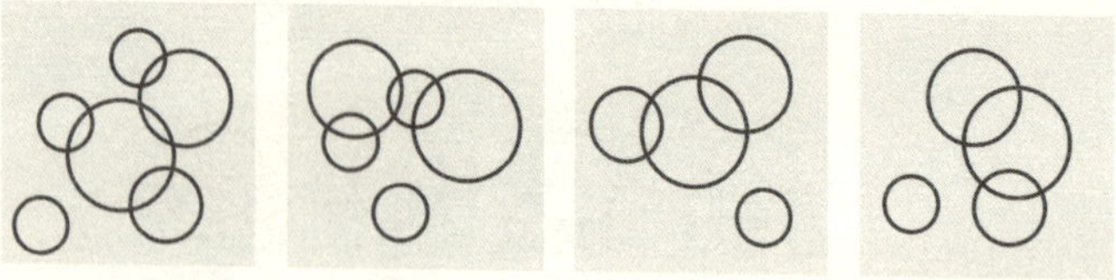

A B C D

28.

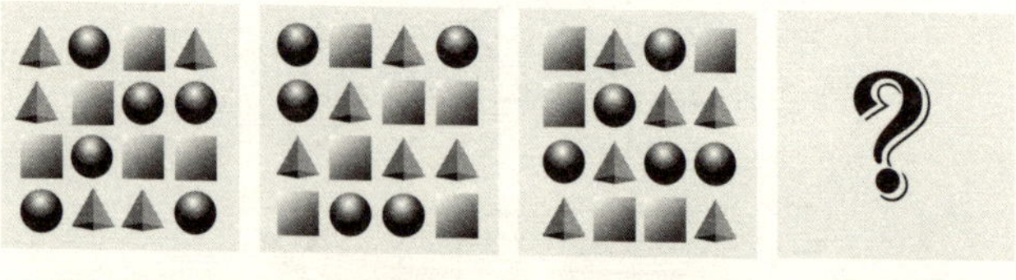

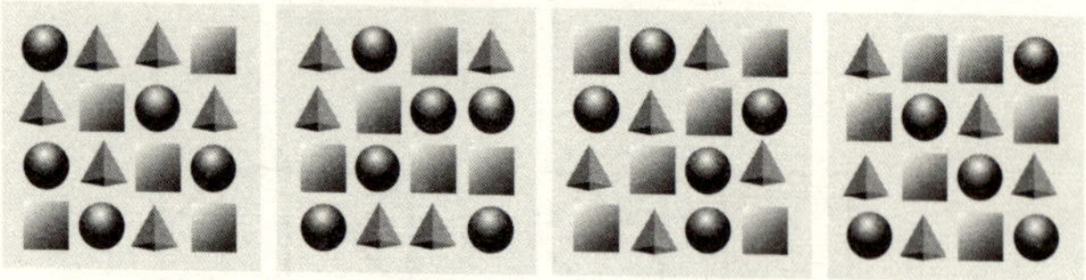

A B C D

29.

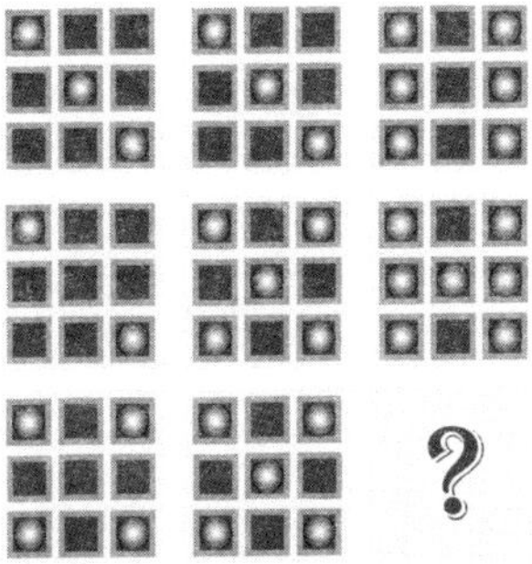

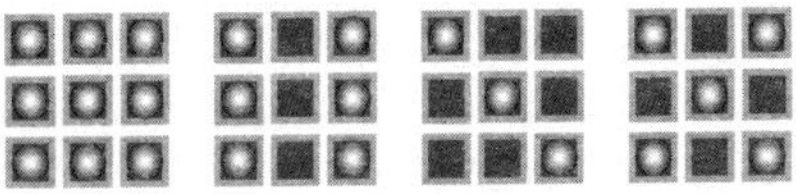

A B C D

30.

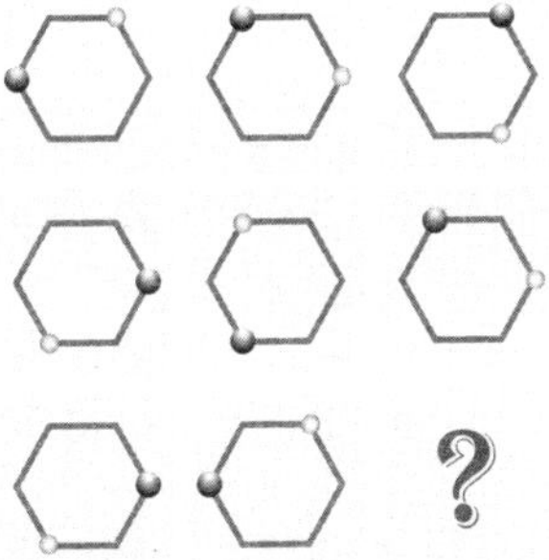

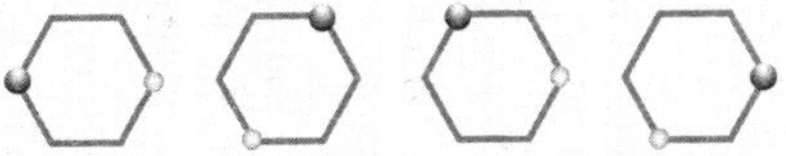

A B C D

Answer key

1. A	11. B	21. D
2. B	12. C	22. D
3. D	13. E	23. B
4. A	14. C	24. D
5. Yes	15. C	25. B
6. Yes	16. C	26. D
7. Yes	17. A	27. B
8. No	18. B	28. B
9. C	19. B	29. A
10. Yes	20. B	30. D

How to score this test

Raw Score	IQ score
1	90
2	92
3	94
4	96
5	98
6	100
7	102
8	104
9	106
10	108
11	110
12	112
13	114
14	116
15	118

Raw Score	IQ score
16	120
17	122
18	124
19	126
20	128
21	130
22	132
23	134
24	136
25	137
26	138
27	139
28	140
29	141
30	142

Interpreting your score

Below you will find a bell curve graph with a range of IQ scores on the bottom and a brief description of each level. The percentages in the curve represent the rarity of such a score in the general population. For example, a score of 115 will put you in the top 16 per cent of the population.

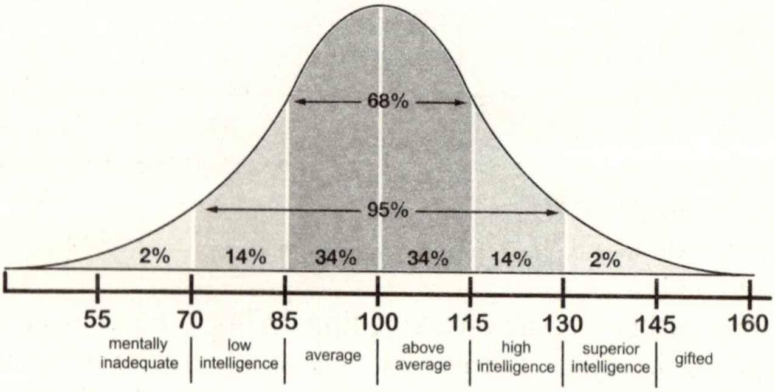

It's important to keep in mind that since this test is not given under controlled conditions, it cannot give a true IQ score. The score given on this test is intended merely as an indicator of how a person might perform on an IQ test.

Postscript and further study

Many psychologists believe IQ tests predict academic and vocational success with moderate efficiency. However, they are not intended to measure other important variables such as abilities responsible for art, music, cooking, mechanical invention, foreign languages, caring for a baby, defeating an enemy in war, and so on. In addition, all professional IQ tests have a degree of error derived from thorough statistical analyses of the standardization sample. It's important to keep in mind that since this test was not given under controlled conditions, and has not gone through rigorous standardizing and normalization, it cannot give a true IQ score. The score given on this test is merely meant to be an indicator of how a person might perform on an IQ test. In short, your obtained score should only be interpreted as a broad estimate of your intelligence.

For further reading on taking timed tests, I recommend *Test Your IQ* by Hans J. Eysenck. The book has several short, timed tests in them that will give you practice with timed tests of this nature.

Appendix I

Levels of intelligence

IQ over 189

In all of human history only about two dozen people have been this smart. William James Sidis is one example. He lectured Harvard mathematicians on four-dimensional mathematics at age 11 and was a professor of mathematics at Rice University at age 14. He easily mastered many more languages than the then "world record" of around 40. He would do the entire New York Times crossword in his head. Because of his eccentricities, academics and the press mercilessly hounded him. At the age of 22 he published a book discussing black holes a full 15 years before Nobel laureate Chandrasekhar thought of them. He eventually refused to do anything academic or have anything to do with academic society. Who knows what these people think about or what they think of the rest of humanity?

IQ 172–188

Keynes – who used to intimidate Bertrand Russell – was probably in this category. John Stuart Mill and Bobby Fischer are also in this category. While still of primary school age only around one-in-a-thousand university professors can look them in the eye intellectually. They tend to read competently before they are three years old. They find even grand system building relatively easy. They are seldom understood or appreciated. Most feel profoundly isolated from society – even when they are appreciated. A large proportion of this group opt out of society and never make revolutionary contributions in the standard academic fields or professions. It seems to be very difficult to motivate them to play the academic/scholarly/professional game because they regard even the most venerable of traditions and institutions as absurd or silly. Consider that their intellect is as far above that of the average person as the average person's intellect is above that of someone with mental retardation. Even the mind of the average professor appears to him like the mind of the average bricklayer would appear to the professor.

IQ 156–172

The smarter Nobel Prize winners and most historical geniuses (people like Einstein, Hawkins, Byron, Milton, Kant, Newton, Russell, Rand) are to be found in this category. Most exceed the average postgraduate in academic competence – even professors – while still in primary school, and probably knew more than their teachers from about the age of eleven. Their powers of comprehension and reason are such that they can see that many alternative systems (theories) account for the essentials inherent in abstract hypotheses and may be able to compare these in turn and bring them within the ambit of a single grand formal system (theory). They can and do read philosophy for pleasure well before puberty. They can read at the university level before the average person can comprehend their first reader, i.e. "I see a cat". They can probably perceive several logically consistent ethical systems and may find themselves struggling with the problem of constructing a grand ethical system. A common experience with people in this category or higher is that they are not wanted – that the masses (including the professional classes) find them an affront of some sort. Fortunately they are plentiful in absolute numbers, so many of them do rise above the envy and hostility. Some teacher, inspiring role model or challenging puzzle manages to interest a few in humanity's theoretical and practical problems. Their IQ is close enough to those in the two categories below them to allow for some communication and influence. They are the source of virtually all of humanity's advances.

IQ 140–156

Most professional mathematicians, physicists, philosophers and high court judges or very senior counsel, can be found in this group. They are autodidacts par excellence. Highly regarded original academic work rarely occurs with lower IQs. Some in this group exceed the average university student in academic competence while still in primary school. They garner most academic honours like Phi Beta Kappa election, Rhodes scholarships, mathematical Olympiads, etc. Many Nobel laureates and some historical geniuses, like Sartre, are also to be found here. Their reasoning powers are sufficient to enable them to build intellectual systems (theories) out of the essential features (not superficialities) of a situation. They can read anything and probably read philosophy for pleasure. Morality is now a matter of self-chosen ethical principles held to a standard of logical consistency. People in this category make up the society's intellectual leaders. Most original ideas start with these people, however their contribution tends to be in bits and pieces rather than a whole new system or new way of seeing things.

IQ 124–140

This group forms the bulk of the better doctors, lawyers, engineers, accountants and other professionals, CEOs of large companies and academics. This category of people and all those above them don't require assistance to learn. They can find the information and master the methods by themselves. They are capable of postgraduate work, including PhDs, but may struggle with a few subjects such as post-graduate mathematics, physics and philosophy. They usually appreciate that abstract hypotheses can be systematized and often attempt to do so (try to form theories), but for the most part they tend to miss the essentials and build systems out of superficialities. Reading philosophy and legal tracts with comprehension is possible. Morality is decidedly a matter of principles for this group but nevertheless they tend to accept established systems, rarely is the principled system a self-chosen one. These people tend to be the keepers, and transmitters, of knowledge and the higher points of any culture, but can't create it themselves.

IQ 108–124

Their best work level is that of most teachers, low- to middle-level management and military officers, substandard to fair professionals and some elected national or provincial politicians. They can learn via the typical university format of lectures and textbooks. At times they might struggle at the university level, but graduation is not difficult. Abstract, what-if hypothetical thinking begins in this group but is still superficial. Some may be aware that their hypotheses could form part of a coherent whole but cannot draw out the whole themselves. Principled morality also begins in this group, i.e. they can see there are non-arbitrary principles or laws that should govern ethical behaviour and thought. They can also see that these laws are social constructs and have not come down from heaven or other ultimate authority. This group makes up the moral, intellectual and practical leadership assistants of society.

IQ 92–108

This is the average person, able to function at the level of skilled blue-collar, clerical, sales or police work. Learning varies from explicit coaching with hands-on experience to study guides and textbook work with some practical experience. They should be able to deal with a secondary school curriculum but quite a few, even with hard work, won't do well enough to enter university. Their reasoning is proficient but pretty concrete at the level of non-essential surface details, and their reading level is, at best, news stories (not editorials), popular magazines and novels. Morality is conventional, a matter of serving the social order and tradition or doing their duty as defined by some authority like the church, a teacher, a parent or the state. This large group is the glue of society but given the wrong authority it (and the two groups below it) may do horrible things in the name of morality.

IQ 76–92

Life is tough at this level. Anything other than unskilled labour is a trial, though simple semi-skilled work is possible. Learning is slow, simple and needs to be supervised closely to be effective. Their reasoning is very superficial and concrete and they cannot see the essential form inherent in many examples of similar things. Most will never be functionally literate and the rest will not understand anything more complex than a popular magazine. It has been estimated that people in this category commit about 75 per cent of all petty and violent crimes. Morality is very much of a primitive conventional sort, i.e. the good is whatever pleases himself or significant others and the bad is anything that displeases him. The vast majority of serious social problems are associated with people in this category because there are so many of them statistically.

IQ 60–76

In the old days, these people used to be called morons or feeble-minded. At least some intermittent outside assistance becomes necessary. At this level and below people are inevitably functionally illiterate even if they have been taught to read for at least four years. Their communication and social skills are reasonable but by social/communication skills I am not referring to negotiation skills or wit, but basics like washing hands, dressing, brushing teeth, using toilet paper, looking at the person addressing them and finding the local doctor. They are socially and vocationally adequate (at menial labour) given special training and supervision. Many are able to lead a relatively independent life. Real (if superficial and concrete) logic appears in this category. Conventional morality also begins to appear in this category, i.e. the good is whatever pleases significant others and the bad anything that displeases them. At this point or below the law begins to regard them as being too stupid to know the difference between right and wrong and won't hold them responsible should they commit a serious crime.

IQ 44–60

Limited support becomes essential. Their social and communication skills are fair but there is little self-awareness. They can function vocationally in a sheltered workshop. They need supervision in their living arrangements and cannot live independently. Their thinking does not involve much in the way of logic. Their ethical thinking is pre-moral, i.e. involves conditioning, but there is the beginning of a quid pro quo sort of morality.

Appendix II

Know Thyself

An essay by Victor Serebriakoff

"Know thyself," said the sage – and this may be the most difficult piece of advice of all. Psychology, man's self-exploring discipline, is accepted as a science in the Anglophone world; but in the Francophone world it is still classed as a branch of philosophy. Philosophers of science agree that to earn its status as a science a subject must come down out of the blurred philosophical clouds to the earth of solidity, rigour, and number.

If any branch of psychology has enough rigour to claim scientific status it is psychometrics, the science of mental measurement.

The pioneer work of Galton, Terman, Burt, Spearman, Binet, Guilford, and Cattell has been consolidated and validated for half a century. There are few serious students of the subject who are prepared to reject the practical value of the mental measurement known as the intelligence test, however much argument there may be about their theoretical basis.

Big industry makes increasing use of them, the educationalist is frankly helpless without them, psychiatrists need them for a proper understanding of their patients, and faith in them and the demand for them by the general project is ever growing.

Are these tests immoral?

Some people cannot square their egalitarian ideals with IQ tests. The very idea of trying to assess human talent and character is anathema – immoral and illegal. To others the innocence and perfectibility of unspoiled man is a quasi-religious doctrine. Marxists are at one with Freud in thinking that all important human differences are environmental, postnatal. Everyman's rights are equal, therefore every man should be equal.

Give me a newborn child, they say, and with the right treatment I will make him a genius. But they do specify a human child. They never ask for a monkey or dog or worm, so perhaps they may think there is something inborn. Even so, attempts were made in all seriousness to apply this doctrine by bringing up a chimpanzee side by side with human children. When they found that the monkey (after a period in the lead) fell behind in mental development they had to conclude that there may be some inherited difference. I expect we shall be told it was caused by choosing a mentally deficient monkey. The Marxists and liberal egalitarian environmentalists, it seems, are confusing the inheritance of wealth with biological inheritance.

Greatly daring, I suspect that if nature rather than nurture is responsible for the difference between men and apes, it might be partly responsible for the difference between the idiot and the genius, though I do not deny that the true human potential is often not fully realized.

A sensible view is that nature sets the ceiling and nurture decides how near to that ceiling we get.

But given the undeniable fact that human beings are unequal in achievement, even if not in potential, we still face the question: "Do we want to know?" Let me argue.

Why we do want to know

In a primitive farming community where everybody toils for survival with simple tools, the advantage of being able to solve sophisticated problems may be little. But that is not how we have chosen to live in Europe and the developed world. The daily continuance of the immensely complex and interrelated commercial and industrial system upon which we depend for the thousand things and services we think we need each day, depends on putting a very large number of round and square human pegs into the proper holes. The continuance of our present civilization depends on finding occupants whose qualities fit closely to an enormous range of highly specified roles. *Home Heart Transplants*, *Do-It-Yourself Brain Surgery*, *Every*

Man His Own Industrial Manager, and *The Amateur Stevedore* are all equally inappropriate book titles. Our complex society works because we have found out how to put the right man or woman into the right job. The fact that we can do this so well is a sign that somewhere or other, seen or unseen, someone is making judgments about what a man can and what he cannot do and what his character is and how bright he is.

We start in the school. We sort and select (and we shall continue to). Despite the partial abandonment of streaming, and the preference for mixed-ability classes, despite Lehrer's satirical slogan: "Rank and position shall be awarded without respect to race, creed, class – or ability," we shall manage to sort people out and use them sensibly and comfortably in accordance with their powers and potentialities. It is safe to predict that all the attempts to abolish the classification of people as to ability will come to nothing. As fast as we throw such "discrimination" out of the door it will creep back in through the window.

At present we "discriminate" by using human judgment, by examinations, by degrees, and by qualifications – which means a lot of senseless "grinding" and education-free "coaching". But, as they become more perfect, we shall use more simple, easily administrated, quick and efficient scientific tests, which are fair, objective, free from nepotism, religious or racial prejudice, influence and the old-boy network. They save time, money, unfairness, unhappiness, and mistakes. Above all, they are predictive.

But these tests are not perfect, they still measure potential inaccurately in the culturally deprived, or in those from cultures different from that on which the tests was standardized, but they are less unfair than anything else. They are only a rough guide, but many experiments have shown that they are better than, and less biased than, unaided human judgment. They are better than guesswork, more efficient than trial and error, and they are improving all the time. They were invented as an instrument of social justice, a way of penetrating to the central capacity of a person despite his lack of education. They are attacked only be egalitarian down-levellers.

There is a great body of experimental evidence that establishes their general validity and very little which contradicts it (though much is made of it by the down-levelling procrusteans, of whom I shall have more to say later).

THE STORY OF INTELLIGENCE TESTS

Intelligence

The first human quality successfully measured was the most important, the one which divides me from the rest of the animal world and which is mankind's biological specialty – intelligence.

What is intelligence? One of the most frequent, obvious, and silly attacks upon intelligence is the dear old "How do you define it?" ploy. This is based on the Euclidian view that nothing is real that cannot be defined. As H.G. Wells pointed out, you can have fun abolishing many classes or concepts by defying people to define them. "Give me," he said, "any definition of a chair or 'chairishness' you please and I will undertake with the aid of a good carpenter to defeat it."

A horse, a clan, a face, happiness, pain, intelligence: we cannot define them so they don't exist, runs the argument.

But what do we mean by intelligence?

Lexicographer Johnson gave the word four senses. The first is commerce of information (mutual communication, distance or secret). The second is commerce of acquaintance (terms on which men live with one another). The third is spirit (unbodied mind). The fourth is the nearest to the modern meaning: "understanding, skill". The modern sense of an inborn quality is altogether missing in Johnson's usage, which deals with acquired powers only.

Spenser shows a glimpse of the modern sense: "Heaps of huge words, unhoarded, hideously, they seem to be cheap praise of poetry; and thereby wanting due intelligence, have marred the face of goodly poesy."

Bacon's phrase could be read either way: "It is not only in order of nature for him to govern that is the more intelligent as Aristotle would have it; but there is not less required for government, courage to protect, and above all, honesty."

In France the pioneer of mental testing, Alfred Binet, used the definition *habileté*, which is fairly close to "ability". But Galton used "intelligence", and the word has come into a new use signifying the inborn problem-solving ability; Galton was the first clearly to establish this by his genetic studies.

The older meaning of the word, "information", has now almost disappeared and the Galton sense is the one usually intended. In other words the common usage derives from the new technical sense and not from the traditional sense of the word. There is, therefore, no legitimate complaint, because "intelligence is what intelligence tests measure". The circularity of this definition is really a feeble joke.

The definition of intelligence in an operational sense is relatively simple. It is demonstrable that the ability of human beings to perform specific tasks varies between one human being and another. It is equally obvious that some people are good at some things and some are good at others. What is not so usually known but is equally true is that there is a relation, or rather a correlation (or measured relation), between skills and abilities. That is to say they are "unfairly" or unequally distributed. There is, alas, no law of compensation as there is popularly supposed to be which ensures that those who are good at one thing are poor at another and vice versa. On the contrary, the tendency is for those who are good at one thing to be good at many and those who are bad at one thing to be bad at many. Thus we get, on the average, a range from the versatile genius who can not only solve problems well but can paint and draw and think and write and even run and jump better than most, to the mentally sub-normal who is below average at the majority of things.

Stop! I know what my beloved reader has started to say here. Wait! I deal with statistical generalizations and not with invariable laws. In the human sciences we are forced to deal with tendencies, not with invariable relations. It is pathetic how frequently otherwise well-educated people feel they have defeated a statement about a statistical tendency by giving one contrary example. "You say," they retort with scorn, "that children who are good at verbal understanding tend to be good at arithmetic – but I can prove you completely wrong; my Johnny is always top in English but he is useless at arithmetic. So there!" Useless to point out that one specifically chosen case does not constitute a sample of great statistical reliability.

Let it be clear that IQ testing lives in the real world of indeterminacy and adopts the simple biological strategy of "the best guess", leaving the unreal determinist world of invariable relations to the philosophers, logicians, and mathematicians who invented it and who still sustain it against all the evidence.

So my operational definition is simply this: "Intelligence is a factor which varies between individuals and is associated with the general level of ability displayed in performing a wide variety of different tasks."

Intelligence in this sense is measurable with reasonable accuracy, and it is a strong indication of the general ability or versatility of the subject. It is not simply a measure of your skill at intelligence tests, it is a measure of something definite and fundamental about you which affects and informs everything you do. Intelligence is not a virtue. Since it is largely genetic, it is nothing to be proud of. But it is not a fault either, and nothing to be ashamed of.

A further definition of intelligence

At the risk of making confusion worse confounded I would like to add another to the many general definitions of intelligence. I prefer the simple operational one, but for the semanticists and lexicographers who are still obsessed with the idea that human concepts can be entrapped and held within the confines of a precise verbal definition I add the following.

Intelligence is a biological phenomenon. It is evident in any living thing or system, however primitive. The universe is dispersing, breaking down, and moving from states of greater to lesser order by the ubiquitous increase of entropy; but it contains a number of self-ordering homeostatic entities which act as though they oppose the universal trend to move from order to disorder, from states of low to higher probability. In this class of entities there is a trend to build up order, to retain stability and to resist changes in form, to preserve low probability and even to lower it. This is the class of living things.

In order to resist the action of the change-forces in the universe these entities have to detect and counteract them. Since the process of counteraction often takes time, these entities have also to be able to predict change-threatening forces, and to do this they have to have sense organs and receive information from the outside universe. They have to store it (in coded form) and transduce it into an appropriate output of instructions to their parts, organs and muscles so that they can resist the tendency of the universe to change their form beyond the level which they can correct. If the change passes beyond this level then a runaway change called death (or decay) sets in.

I define intelligence therefore as a capacity in an entity (living thing or artifact) to detect, encode, store, sort and process signals generated in the universe and transduce them into an optimal output pattern of instructions. The word "optimal" may cause some difficulty here because that is where "value" creeps in. I would define it as that which is best designed in the longest-term sense to ensure the preservation of the form of the entity concerned through time. It would include "evolutionary" changes in that form, i.e. those which tended to make the entity an even better homeostatic form-preserving device. It may be thought that my definition creates more difficulties than it solves, but there it is for what it is worth.

If we accept it, then the measurement of intelligence would be associated with a number of parameters of the described process. High intelligence would be associated with a large store of information, accuracy of coding, accessibility of information, long-term prediction, accuracy of probability estimates and ability to generate emergent or original behavioral solutions to problems.

Testing general and special ability

The discovery that abilities correlate was crucial. It led to the notion that there is some general factor underlying the individual differences and contributing to a person's success in a number of skills. Thus Spearman accounted for both the individual variations of skill and the tendency for abilities to "cluster" in certain people. His "theory" is really a simple conceptual framework which helps us to think about human ability more clearly. Each person can be assessed for "g" (general-ability" and "s" (special-ability) factors. In any one particular skill your "g" rating contributes part and your "s" rating the rest of your score.

If you have a high "g" and a high "s" for, say, music, then you will probably be a better musician than if you have the high "s" score with a low "g" score.

The only way to get at "g" is by using a number of different tests each of which is a partial test of "g". That is why we have batteries of different tests. Each type of test has a different "g" saturation or "loading," and the verbal ability has the highest "g" saturation. Most tests reflect this.

A well-designed intelligence test should not, of course, test the educational background of the subject. Even the verbal test items are usually chosen to avoid those that would be more likely to be known to a well-educated person. It is the ability of the subject to discern the exact shade of meaning of relatively common words which is measured, and not his knowledge of esoteric ones like "esoteric."

Are IQ tests reliable?

Strangely enough, the idea of measuring reliability first arose from a consideration of the difficulties of intelligence testing. To what extent do test results repeat themselves? There is a test-retest variation and one of the methods used to sort out good tests from bad tests is to check it. An average deviation of 5 or 6 points is not unusual and the further from the average the score, the greater the variation is likely to be.

The regression to the mean

A little-understood phenomenon is the regression to the mean. Those around the average have an equal chance of being higher or lower when tested again, but those who get a very high score tend to get a lower one on retesting and those with a very low score a higher one. There is no mystery about this. In order to make tests administratively practical they have to be simple to mark. There should be a limited number of answers from which the subject must choose. They are closed-ended. When they are arranged in this style they can be marked by any clerk or even by a computer. If the questions are open-ended, i.e. when there are many possible valid answers and not all are listed, then only a highly trained specialist can decide between them; even then it is necessary for him to be of higher intelligence than those he tests. Now when we are using closed-ended tests with a limited number of answers it is possible for a well-trained monkey to get a score by going through and guessing at random. If there are five possible answers he would get one in five right on average. Therefore every test result is part luck and part intelligence. They are so arranged that the luck element is small, but it is there. The probability of getting a high score is very low, but if we test a large number of people, as we do, then someone will win that particular sweepstake. So among any high-scoring group there will be a certain number who have had both luck and skill, and the higher the score the greater the chance that luck has contributed something toward it. Similarly, the lower the score the greater the chance that bad luck has contributed to it. On retesting, therefore, the frequency of a repetition of good luck or bad luck will (in a large sample) be low. Therefore the probability is that scores will tend back toward the average.

Culture contamination

To what extent are intelligence tests fair to everybody? Measuring intelligence is an inferential process. We know of no way to probe the communication pathways of the brain and assess their general power to process information and transduce it into action. We have to base our conclusions on the behaviour and treat the brain as a "black box", whose properties we can only learn by inference.

Matters are further confused by the fact that every individual goes through a different set of experiences from the moment of birth, and since the brain is the most efficient device known for sensing and being conditioned by external influences, what it is at any given moment is very much affected by what has happened to it up until that moment.

To get at the inborn (the genetic) qualities, we have to penetrate three layers. From the external behaviour we can infer the internal mental efficiency, which is decided by a combination of the inherent qualities and external environmental experiences. From the second layer – mental efficiency – we have to deduce the third and deepest layer – inherent or inborn capacity. Professor Raymond Cattell distinguishes sharply between what he calls "fluid" and "crystallized" intelligence. The former corresponds to the inborn capacity, the potentiality, the ceiling which cannot be transcended. "Crystallized" intelligence corresponds to the measurable problem-solving abilities, the capacity to deal with information and produce appropriate behaviour, or to make ticks in the right places on an IQ test.

Most psychologists believe that an intelligence test is only valid inside a given culture. Wherever you have a large number of children brought up speaking the same language and living in the same background of ideas and books and experiences, there is sufficient similarity in their environmental background that tests can be devised which can sort the children into classes which are associated with their genetic potential. But even the best tests, it is claimed, are culture contaminated; if we test people brought up in one cultural background – say, southern black children in America – by tests devised and standardized on those from another cultural background – say, American children as a whole – then we shall get a low reading from the former group. Of all the attacks upon intelligence tests this is the most valid.

By a corollary, intelligence tests cannot be used to gauge the relative intelligence of different ethnic or cultural groups. It is easy to standardize a test for each individual group and to find a mean and a standard deviation for that group. It is quite another to relate the different means and standard deviations to each other. There is some dispute in the world of psychometrics about whether and how this problem can be overcome.

Some psychometricians like Cattell have produced "culture-free" tests which are claimed to be equally fair to those of all cultural groups, and there is considerable evidence that this may be so. Other psychometricists claim that these culture-free tests are weighted in favour of a certain type of intelligence and ignore other important aspects. I pointed out earlier that most pyschometricists agree that this has what they call the greatest "g" loading, that is, the highest association with the general ability factor which they are trying to measure. Unfortunately, it is this very ability which cannot be tested appropriately by "culture-free" tests since any language items must favour the language group of the language chosen. (It might be thought that language items can easily be translated, but the subtleties of semantic difference between different languages are such that a straightforward translation would be quite inappropriate.)

The distribution of intelligence

Like many other human qualities, intelligence is "normally" distributed. That is to say, if we put people into "intelligence" classes according to how bright they are, there will be a large number near the average. These will tail off in the typical Gaussian or bell curve, as people do for height or weight or any other variable human quality (see next page).

The Gaussian curve was derived from the theory of errors. It is the kind of curve produced by examining the variations of measurements of entities affected by a large number of random variables. It is the kind of curve that would be expected on a polygenic explanation of the heredity of intelligence. That is to say, it is the curve that would be produced if intelligence depended upon a number of genes and not just on one.

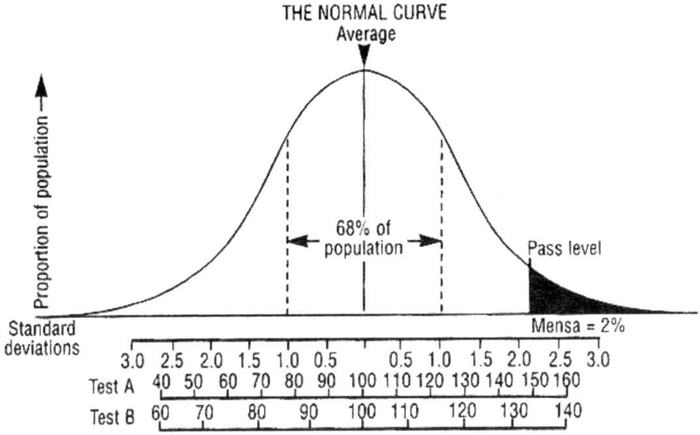

A lot has been made of this normal distribution; perhaps too much, because a careful examination of the theoretical work which led to intelligence tests shows that the original experimenters started with the assumption of normal distribution and made this the test of their results' validity. The fact that they come out at the end with what they put in at the beginning is hardly surprising. Nonetheless, it is a fairly safe assumption and should be looked upon as a good working rule rather than an experimental conclusion. There would be a good case for saying, "Let us assume normal distribution until we have evidence to the contrary." Some evidence to the contrary is already visible at the lower end of the scale, as might be expected. With any complicated entity like a human being there are more things that can render it imperfect than there are things that can improve it. Evidence exists that there are two swellings to the curve of the low tail. One may represent birth damage; the other is as yet unexplained. The fact that this does not emerge from all intelligence-test data is due to the fact that cretins, idiots, and morons tend not to get into our original samples.

Taking the Gaussian curve to its logical conclusion, we would expect intelligence to extend infinitely in the upward direction. Also, at two standard deviations we get about two per cent, at three, one in a thousand, and so on ad infinitum. But it seems unlikely to me that the curve would hold good for many standard deviations.

The ceiling

A series of experiments with mice has shown that there appears to be a biological ceiling for the development of intelligence. Two groups of mice were bred apart as regards their ability to learn to run mazes; the quickest learners were bred together and so were the slowest. In a relatively small number of generations the two populations were so different that the slowest of the fast-learners group learned faster than the fastest of the slow learners. But further selection from the brightest of the bright produced no improvement, as it soon became evident that in a given stock of mice there was a natural limit to further development. My guess is that there is a similar ceiling to human intelligence. The analogy is a poker game. You shuffle your cards and everyone gets a hand; your particular hand is a matter of chance, and the probability of getting a royal flush is fairly low but it is predictable. By manipulating the pack and taking out some cards, you can increase the chances of a high hand but you cannot get anything higher than a royal flush – except by a miracle. There is a Russian story that the Apostles and Christ were playing cards: when the payoff came, Peter produced three queens, and Mark four kings and Paul put down a royal flush and turning to Christ said, "Now then, none of your bloody miracles." For our purpose we must read "miracle" as a new combination of mutations. The more complex a species gets, the less likely an improving combination is. So we may have to wait some time for a bloody miracle. Meanwhile we could, if we wanted to, arrange that more people get high hands in the genetic poker game, or we could reduce the number of low hands. But that is a new and highly controversial subject which I will have the wisdom to leave at this point, otherwise someone will say "Hitler" or "eugenics" or some other swear word and all rational thought will cease.

SPEED

The tester tested

Another chestnut of the anti-testers is the false paradox: "How does the tester deal with people more intelligent than he is?" The answer is a question of speed. The brighter you are, the faster you solve problems, even simple ones. That is why nearly all intelligence tests are "speeded". That is to say, they are deliberately designed not to give the subject sufficient time. Many of those who complain because they cannot pass the Mensa tests say, "I didn't have enough time." Of course they didn't. Any test which gave everyone sufficient time would do a poor job of discrimination. However, there is some argument about this among psychometricians, and there are other types of tests called "power" tests in which what is tested is the ability to solve difficult problems: people are divided into categories according to their ability to solve them at all. It is much more difficult to devise this kind of test; they have to be much more carefully graded for difficulty and sorted into order of difficulty in the test. I agree from many years' experience in developing Mensa that there is something in this. But it may be difficult to produce a really convincing experiment to demonstrate the fact, if fact it is.

Dr. Furneaux of the Maudsley Institute holds a different view and has produced a theory of testing which is based purely on the time the subject takes to solve a large number of relatively simple items. This leads to the possibility of a mental testing machine, and some experiments in this have indeed been made.

Test sophistication

Even though test times are chosen with particular care to avoid it, there is obviously a practice effect – the more tests you do, the better you do them. In a properly validated test, however, the change in the score that can be made by practice is not great (about 5 or 6 points). It reaches a ceiling after a few trials and does not improve further.

Professor Eysenck has proposed that since so many people

are getting intelligence-test practice it would be wise to absorb this cause of fluctuation by giving every child practice. The present book might be looked upon as a mean to this end. On the other hand, the process of giving "training" in IQ tests is to be deplored if it takes time from real education. Also, children who achieve academic opportunities after such "training" might displace more promising ones who had not. This would obviously not be fair.

One of the most frequent questions to Mensa is whether it makes any difference to the result if the subject is unwell, has the flu, was drunk, tired, menstruating, or was depressed when he or she took the test. The answer is that it does not make nearly as much difference as people think. Experiments show that temporary temperament is not a very big cause of variation. I hate to rob people of such a comfort when they do badly, so my advice is: wait till you have a headache, then take your test – it will give you a slightly conservative estimate, which is good for your ego if you are bright, and it will enable you to kid yourself that the results are not meaningful if you are not and cannot take it.